ta___t

for life & love

THE HIGH PRI...

WHEEL of FORTUNE

tarot
for life & love

using the tarot to get the most out of relationships

Jane Struthers

Kyle Cathie Limited

With much love for my dear friends, the Genthners:
Zen Master Dae Gak, Mara, Maggie, Gretchen and Sam

THE STAR

Acknowledgements

It can seem as though a book is the sole product of its author and no one else is involved in its creation. Yet all the best books are a joint effort between many people, who all contribute their own particular talents. Well, that is what every author hopes for, even if they do not get it. So I consider myself to be extremely lucky in having worked on this book with such a fabulous team of people. Thanks to everyone at Kyle Cathie who worked on the book, but especially to Kyle Cathie for her enthusiastic support; Caroline Taggart for being such the ideal, constructive editor; and Sarah Epton for her good-natured and skilful editing. Many, many thanks, too, to Robert Updegraff who has once again designed a delicious-looking book. Last but not least, thanks to my agent, Chelsey Fox, for all her involvement, and my husband, Bill Martin, for his loving encouragement.

First published in Great Britain in 2002 by
Kyle Cathie Limited • 122 Arlington Road • London NW1 7HP
general.enquiries@kyle-cathie.com
www.kylecathie.com

ISBN 978 1 85626 809 7

Text © 2002 by Jane Struthers

Editor Caroline Taggart
Editorial Assistant Sarah Epton
Designer Robert Updegraff
Production by Lorraine Baird and Sha Huxtable
Illustrations from Universal-Waite Tarot Deck reproduced by permission of US Games Systems, Inc., Stamford, CT 06902 USA. Copyright © 1990 by US Games Systems, Inc. Further reproduction prohibited.

Jane Struthers is hereby identified as the author of this work in accordance with Section 77 of the Copyright, Designs and Patents Act 1988.

A Cataloguing in Publication record for this title is available from the British Library.

Printed in China through Colorcraft Ltd., Hong Kong

contents

introduction

'I love mankind – it's people I can't stand.' So said Charles M. Schultz in one of his wonderful *Peanuts* cartoons. Many of us have experienced a challenging relationship in which we cannot live apart yet it is equally hard to live together. Even when we are in a fulfilling partnership, it is easy to allow our day-to-day lives to be entirely coloured by the quality of that relationship. When things are going well, we are sunny and cheerful. We feel protected from harm, cosy and safe. Life is wonderful. However, if we have a row over breakfast with our beloved or our children, and then go off to work in high dudgeon, we may take out our bad mood on everyone we bump into that day, or feel completely abandoned and wretched. It can seem as though life has little to offer us.

If we are honest and are prepared to acknowledge some necessary truths, we can learn the greatest lessons about ourselves from the many different people in our lives. This means everyone we come into contact with, from the postman to our colleagues, our parents to our partners, our best friend to our worst enemy. We may see all sorts of admirable traits in other people that we are completely unaware of in ourselves. For instance, we might respect our friends for their kindness and compassion without realising that we, too, have these same qualities. Equally, we can be unconscious of some of our more difficult features, while seeing them vividly in other people. We might complain about how rude people are to us, totally ignorant of the fact that we can be pretty unpleasant ourselves sometimes. We may even unwittingly provoke people into being offensive, for a variety of reasons of which we are not always aware.

holding up the mirror

Sometimes it is very difficult to see what is happening, especially when we are caught in the grip of intense emotions or profound fears. We may also be acting unknowingly, so we are blissfully ignorant of our behaviour. This is where the tarot can be so useful, because it holds up a mirror to the situation about which we need guidance and reflects it back to us. It reveals what is really going on, often with astonishing clarity and breathtaking accuracy. It is also totally objective, and it does not pull its punches. The tarot always shows us how things really are.

The seventy-eight cards that comprise the tarot illustrate many different situations, motives and emotions. They are especially effective at explaining the dynamics of a relationship because they can not only reveal how we are feeling but will also describe the state of mind of whoever else is involved. This is particularly useful in relationships that involve a great deal of stress, animosity or tension. These are usually the most highly-charged and painful situations, so we can find plenty of reasons for not wanting to look at them too closely. We might be very reluctant to have a face-to-face conversation with someone who is causing us problems, and so we are left in the dark about their motives or their side of the story. We can only guess, or make assumptions that may or may not be correct. However, if we use the tarot to examine our feelings, or to explore a particular sticking point, we will gain valuable insights into what is happening. These will show us how to approach the problem and do our best to improve it. They will also indicate what we are currently bringing to the situation and what more we can offer.

The tarot contains some uncompromising messages, not only about other people but also about ourselves. If we are willing to learn from it, we will discover some very useful lessons about the roles that we play in our relationships. Almost inevitably, some of these will make us feel happy and others less so. But it is important to accept and acknowledge every facet of our personalities that is revealed to us through the tarot, because by bringing these into awareness we stand a better chance of having some control over them. We may also discover some wonderful nuggets of gold within ourselves, as we unearth our own hidden treasure chests of gifts and potential.

asking difficult questions

This book has been specially written to show how the tarot can help you to understand your relationships, in all their many guises, and also to be aware of the part that you play in them. The interpretations of the cards discuss their classic meanings and go on to explore these in greater depth within the context of your own situation.

Some of these interpretations may ask awkward or uncomfortable questions because they are intended to help you explore your situation in detail and with honesty. They hold up the mirror to your relationships and you may not always like what you see. Yet you will find it immensely valuable if you can listen to what the tarot is saying, whether it makes you want to break open the champagne because it brings such wonderful news or tempts you to go back to bed and pull the covers over your head. It will always help you to gain further insight into what is going on and enable you to learn from it. The tarot really can help you to find greater satisfaction in your life.

the history of the tarot

It is impossible to describe the early history of the tarot with any accuracy because there are so many conflicting theories. Some sources claim that it began in ancient Egypt, others that it was a Romany method of divination that originated in Spain. The situation was not helped in medieval Europe by the need to disguise the tarot's many references to what were then considered to be dangerous and subversive beliefs and practices, such as paganism and Catharism. At a time when heretics were burnt at the stake and a fundamentalist version of Christianity was spreading like wildfire, an interest in the tarot must have almost amounted to a death sentence. The images on the cards were made deliberately complex in order to fox people who were not initiated into the mysteries of the tarot, and contained references to the kabbalah, numerology, astrology and freemasonry, as well as other disciplines that would only be obvious to people in the know.

The oldest surviving tarot cards were painted in Italy in the fifteenth century for the Colleoni family. Not long afterwards, in France, B. P. Grimaud created the Marseilles deck, which is still used today. At the time, it was extremely influential throughout Europe, not only in its images and names for the cards but also its high production values (such as being printed on heavier, more durable paper) which were eventually adopted for other decks.

The tarot enjoyed a resurgence of popularity in the late nineteenth and early twentieth centuries, and one of the most significant decks to appear during that time was the Rider-Waite pack, which was first published in 1909. The Universal Waite Tarot, which provides all the illustrations in this book, is a more colourful version of the original Rider-Waite deck.

In recent years, the tarot has experienced another explosion of activity, leading to a wide range of different decks. Ironically, religious fundamentalism is also enjoying a revival, with various influential groups of people becoming increasingly suspicious of such disciplines as astrology and the tarot.

the Major and Minor Arcana

The tarot consists of seventy-eight cards, which are divided into two sections: the Major and Minor Arcana. Together, they describe virtually every experience we are likely to meet in life, such as birth and death, marriage and separation, beginnings and endings, friendship and enmity, prosperity and impoverishment. This basic format of the tarot has not changed since it first became popular in Renaissance Europe.

the Major Arcana

The Major Arcana comprises twenty-two cards which are always illustrated, and which describe a person's path through life. With all the stages that are encountered along the way, this can be viewed as a journey of initiation or self-discovery.

Each card corresponds with a planet or astrological sign. Some also contain archetypal figures, such as the Magician and the Hermit, and these tend to represent particular characters that we all meet in life. The illustrations on each card include symbols that expand on the meaning of that particular card and act as triggers to your unconscious, prompting interpretations that go much deeper than the surface messages. As you become more proficient with the tarot, and more confident about using it, you will be delighted by the increasing depth and richness of your readings.

the Minor Arcana

The Minor Arcana consists of fifty-six cards, divided into four suits of fourteen cards each: Cups, Wands, Swords and

Pentacles. The Minor Arcana is believed to be the precursor to ordinary playing cards, and there are links between the meanings of their suits: Cups correspond with Hearts, Wands with Clubs, Swords with Spades, and Pentacles with Diamonds. In addition to ten 'pip' cards, there are four court cards, whereas there are only three in each suit of ordinary playing cards. In some decks, the pip cards carry an illustration and in others they simply feature the number in a similar way to ordinary playing cards.

The Minor Arcana portray the mundane details of our existence. The pip cards describe the various stages that we meet in life, from the inception of an idea or venture, through its challenges, to its completion. The court cards have a dual meaning because they can refer either to a situation or a person. When several appear in a spread they indicate that other people are involved, either directly or by trying to have some influence over what is happening.

cups This suit rules the realms of emotions and love, in all their forms. It therefore governs relationships between friends, colleagues and relatives as well as lovers. Cups are associated with all forms of creativity and fertility, whether this is the birth of a child, the development of a talent or the abundance of nature. They also rule the unconscious, and correspond to the astrological element of water, so tend to have links with people born under the signs of Cancer, Scorpio and Pisces. An emphasis on Cups in a spread indicates that the questioner, or person having the reading, is very emotionally involved in the situation and may therefore lack objectivity.

wands Wands are connected with travel, whether it is mental, spiritual or physical. There is usually a lot of speculation and optimism about such journeys. Negotiations, adventures, gambles, risks, innovations, dreams and visions all come under the aegis of this suit. Wands also govern the central themes of one's life, such as putting your family first, ambition, or pursuing a creative path. They correspond to the astrological element of fire, so may have links with people born under the signs of Aries, Leo and Sagittarius. An emphasis on Wands in a spread indicates that the questioner is willing to take chances, and actually may be tempted to take more risks than is sensible.

swords Like some of their physical counterparts, Swords are double-edged. They rule words and thoughts, which can be positive or negative. For instance, they govern bright ideas as well as worries, and both truth and lies. They are connected with all forms of mental and intellectual activity, and all types of communication, such as letters, telephone calls and conversations. Swords are immensely logical and rational. They correspond to the astrological element of air, so may have links with people born under the signs of Gemini, Libra and Aquarius. An emphasis on Swords in a spread indicates that the questioner is unduly worried about the situation and may be giving it more thought than it deserves. They may also imagine that a problem is worse than it really is.

pentacles Pentacles are connected with all material matters, such as money, property, business, career and status, as well as anything else that is of value to the questioner. They are firmly rooted in physical reality, so govern things that we can see, touch and hold, rather than anything that can only be imagined. They therefore rule the five senses. This suit also controls practical commitments and daily, routine work. Pentacles correspond to the astrological element of earth, so may have links with people born under the signs of Taurus, Virgo and Capricorn. An emphasis on Pentacles in a spread suggests that the questioner should adopt a more matter-of-fact approach to the situation, and deal with what is actually happening to them rather than getting caught up in what they want, or think, should happen.

using the tarot

The tarot is not nearly as frightening or daunting as it can seem if you have never read it before. It is easy to be alarmed by the prospect of learning the meanings of all the cards in the deck, and even more sobering to think that you then have to put them together to make a coherent reading. But all this comes with practice. What is important is to get a feel for the cards and to take your time with them. Gradually, they will become friends and you will have an instinctive understanding of what each one means.

which tarot deck to buy?

There are many tarot decks to choose from. You can opt for something traditional, such as the Rider-Waite, Marseilles or Visconti-Sforza decks, or a contemporary one that is linked with a particular theme, such as Wicca, Arthurian legend or animals. If you are just beginning your relationship with the tarot, you may find it easiest to start with a traditional deck so you can fix the classic meanings of the cards in your mind, without being distracted by subsidiary themes or illustrations. Later on, you can graduate to something that has special significance for you. Do not feel that you have to choose a deck because it is the 'proper' one or because your friends use it. The best one for you is the one that you feel most comfortable with, and this may change over the years.

Some of the considerations to take into account, which may not occur to you when you are gazing at a multitude of decks in a shop, is whether the cards will fit your hand. Large cards can be very dramatic and exciting, but not always easy to shuffle. They also tend to take up a substantial amount of space when you are laying them out into spreads. Circular cards are unusual and attractive, but you may find it difficult to riffle them when shuffling and also hard to form them into a neat stack.

As the tarot has gained in popularity over the years it has become easier to find a good selection of decks in bookshops. You can also buy them over the Internet through the many websites devoted to the tarot, and some sites even offer sample readings using a selection of decks, so you can experiment and see which one most appeals to you.

becoming familiar with the tarot

When you have chosen your deck, you can begin to enjoy yourself with it. It will respond most effectively if you keep using it, as you will impregnate it with your energy. Get accustomed to handling the cards, and study all of them in detail, so that you become familiar with them. As you read each interpretation in this book, look at the relevant card so you can start to combine its meaning with its illustration. In this way, you will get a good sense of what each one represents.

Sometimes you can buy second-hand decks cheaply, but it can be difficult to acclimatise yourself to them. You may find that they give strange readings or that you do not really enjoy using them even though you like the designs of the cards themselves. The most effective way to deal with this is to cleanse the deck of any residual energy left by its previous owner, which you can do quite simply by holding all the cards between your palms and imagining that they are being bathed in a pure, white light that has been sent from a higher power. You may want to call this Divine energy, or God, or simply think of it as a source of supreme, spiritual power. Imagine the light completely cleansing all the cards; you may have to repeat the process if they do not respond in the way you want. This is also a good technique to use if you want to clean the deck after a particularly difficult reading, or after it has been handled by someone who makes you feel uncomfortable.

storing the cards

The manner in which you store your tarot cards is a cause of great debate. You might like to protect them against negative energies by wrapping them in a piece of purple silk and storing them in a wooden box when they are not in use. This gives a sense of ritual to your readings, and reminds you to treat your cards with respect. You can also lay them out on the piece of silk, if it is large enough. Alternatively, you can keep the cards in the packet in which they were sold, although this may not be as aesthetically pleasing and is unlikely to invoke much feeling of ritual. The packaging may also get rather battered and torn with repeated use, and there is then a danger of losing or damaging some of the contents.

practice makes perfect

Once you have become familiar with the cards, you are ready to move on to the next step and give a reading. It is a good idea to practise on yourself first, so you can get into the routine. Say everything out loud, as though someone else were in the room,

because this will give you confidence when you come to read
the cards for other people. Incidentally, it can be just as
effective to give yourself a reading as it is to receive it from
someone else. However, you must try to remain objective when
interpreting any difficult cards. Don't be tempted to gloss over
them or even ignore them altogether, as this will defeat the
whole point of the reading.

giving a reading

What follows is the basic framework for conducting a reading. It
may seem like a lot to remember at first, but as you become
more accustomed to the procedure it will become second nature.

make the questioner feel comfortable

When giving a reading to someone else, who is traditionally
called 'the questioner', do your best to put them at their ease.
They may be feeling nervous about what you will say, or be
desperately hoping that the cards will tell them what they
want to hear. They might also be worried about getting
involved in something that they do not understand, with fears
that they are somehow dabbling in witchcraft. You may have
to reassure them on such points.

Neither of you will be able to relax or concentrate if you are
sitting in a noisy room or surrounded by people who are
curious or sceptical about what is going on. Do your best to
ensure that you will not be disturbed by such intrusions as
doorbells and phone calls.

Almost inevitably, private and sensitive matters are
discussed in tarot readings. Your questioner will want to know
that you will not divulge what is said between you, whether
you are members of the same family, friends, neighbours or
complete strangers. You might therefore like to prepare a
short, standard speech that you can say each time you give a
reading, such as 'What passes between us is confidential and
I will not discuss it with anyone else.' Your questioner may
want to discuss the meeting with other people, but that is up
to them. Your lips should remain sealed, unless you have the
express permission of the questioner to discuss the reading.

Arrange the seating carefully and sensitively. Try to make sure that you are both at the same height: you do not want to unconsciously set up a situation in which your chair is higher than your questioner's and you therefore appear to have more authority. The best readings are usually given when you are both seated at a table, and you can both see the cards clearly. It is difficult to relax if you are craning your neck to read the cards. Make sure the lighting is good: in order to create a calming atmosphere yet one in which the cards are clearly visible, you are striving for a happy medium between depressing gloom and operating-theatre brilliance.

grounding and tuning in

This next step is rarely, if ever, mentioned in tarot books, yet it is very important and will help you to give better, more focused and intuitive readings. Although it sounds like a lengthy process, with practice you can complete it in less than a minute.

Before you give a reading, you should ground yourself, and then attune yourself to higher energies. Grounding is a very simple technique in which you imagine roots growing out of the soles of your feet into the floor. See them going deep down into the earth and connecting you to its energies. If you do this exercise properly, the soles of your feet will become warm and start to tingle. You should then picture yourself being bathed in a warm, refreshing, purifying waterfall, which helps to wash away any negative energies that you may have picked up, and also enables you to relax.

The next step is to attune to higher energies. These are the same energies that you connected with when cleansing your tarot deck (see page 13). Visualise a beam of light coming down to you and entering the crown of your head from the highest point you can conceive. If you wish, you can also silently ask for spiritual guidance during the reading. The more grounded you are, the better your intuition will be. Finally, you must protect yourself from negative energies by imagining that you are surrounded by a bubble of light.

If you do not want to tell your questioner exactly what you are doing, you can simply inform them that you are preparing yourself for the reading and then shut your eyes for a minute or so while you go through this process.

asking the question

The tarot is not about guessing games or displaying your psychic abilities by telling the questioner what is on their mind. Instead, you should gently ask them what they want to explore with the help of the tarot cards. Some people will be more forthcoming than others, so do not be offended if someone gives you a minimal amount of information. Make sure you understand the nature of their question, because then you can interpret the cards accordingly.

choosing a suitable spread

When you understand the nature of the question, you can decide which spread to use. For instance, if the questioner wants to take an overview of their situation, you might choose the Celtic Cross or the Horoscope Spread. You can then follow this, if necessary, with a more detailed reading that examines what came up in the first one.

The choice of spread also depends on your expertise. There is no point in trying something that is beyond your abilities because it is too complicated or esoteric. When you are starting to learn the tarot, you will be most successful if you stick to relatively simple spreads, such as the Horseshoe. You can then move on to more complicated examples, such as the Pyramid, when you feel more confident.

Whichever spread you choose, it must be capable of answering the question sensibly. For instance, if it is an either-or question, such as 'Should I leave my wife or stay with her and move house?', you cannot use a spread that is designed to answer only one question. In fact, you may not be able to find a spread that caters for each facet of the question so, instead, you may have to break the question down into its component parts, starting with 'Should I leave my wife?' Actually, it would be wiser to reframe this question to 'What will happen if I leave my wife?' or 'I would like insight into my relationship with my wife', because words like 'should' and 'ought' can stir up all sorts of moral dilemmas that are not the province of the tarot. They may also touch on your own principles, which might not match those of your questioner. Tarot readers who believe that their own ethical or moral code is the only one that is 'right', and that everyone else should abide by it, are on a hiding to nothing.

creating your own spreads

If you cannot find a suitable spread that will answer someone's question, you can invent your own. This is much simpler than it may sound, but it does need some preliminary thought. First of all, make sure you have understood the question so you know how to answer it. For instance, if you want to examine the outcomes of two different options, you should create card positions for each one, such as 'the benefits', 'the pitfalls' and 'the outcome'. Make sure you jot down the meaning of each card's position so you do not forget these later on when you come to interpret them.

You can also create very simple three-card spreads with such categories as 'past', 'present' and 'future', or 'morning', 'afternoon' and 'evening' if you want to examine a single day. Spreads do not have to be complicated to be effective, so do not worry about inventing something that seems very basic. It may turn out to be a spread that you use time and again, because it works so well for you.

shuffling the cards

When you have decided which spread to use, and you know what the question is, or the general framework of the reading if it is being kept deliberately vague, your questioner is ready to shuffle the cards. Encourage them to do this for as long as they want while thinking of their question.

The process of shuffling the deck enables the questioner's energies to merge with those of the cards, and also allows the cards to pick up the question that is in the person's mind. Ideally, both of you should remain silent while this is going on, so you can focus your thoughts.

If any cards fall out of the deck at this stage, make a mental note of them and then replace them in the deck. They may have a particular relevance that will become apparent during the reading.

When the questioner has shuffled the cards, they can cut the deck into two or three piles and then reassemble these in a different order before handing back the cards. Alternatively, they may prefer to give you the shuffled deck without cutting it, depending on their mood. Again, there is no right or wrong method, so do not worry if your questioner does not want to cut the pack.

dealing out the cards

Deal out the cards from the top of the deck into the pattern of the spread you have chosen. You can place them face-down if you enjoy the dramatic impact of turning them over once they have all been laid out, or you may prefer to deal them face-up in the first place. You will have to turn all the cards the correct way up before starting the reading anyway, so that you can gain an overall impression of the spread. Try to keep your opinions to yourself at this stage. Your questioner will probably be nervous and worried about what the cards are going to say, so it will not help if you draw in your breath sharply when you spot a difficult or exciting card, or make any other indication of what you are thinking.

reversed cards

Sometimes, when you deal out the cards a few of them will be upside down. These are known as reversed cards. Some tarot readers give special significance to such cards, believing that their position indicates that their meaning has also been reversed or altered in some way. Therefore, difficult cards become more positive when reversed, and vice versa. Other tarot readers believe that a reversed card indicates a delay in whatever it suggests will happen. Examples or explanations of reversed cards are not included in this book because my interpretation of each card includes both positive and negative meanings. When I give readings, I ignore reversed cards, preferring to turn them round so they are in their upright positions.

assessing the spread

Before you launch into the reading, take an overview of the spread. This not only allows you to see if any themes, such as change, are emphasised but also gives your intuition time to start working. Count up the Major Arcana cards, to see whether you have an average number of them. There are two-and-a-half Minor Arcana cards to every Major Arcana card, so in a spread of ten cards you would expect to see four from the Major Arcana. If there are more, destiny is somehow at work and the questioner may find that much of what happens is beyond their control. If there are fewer than average, the solution to the problem is within the jurisdiction of the questioner.

You should also count up the different suits of the Minor Arcana, since a predominance of a particular suit will be significant. A large number of court cards in a spread, for instance, indicates that other people are involved in the situation, and they may even be interfering in what is going on.

starting the reading

After you have gained an overview of the spread, you are ready to interpret each card in turn. Do this systematically, starting with the first and working through to the last. If, in the middle of your reading, inspiration suddenly dawns about an additional meaning for one of the cards you have already read, mention it sooner rather than later so you do not forget it. However, both you and the questioner will get confused if your reading darts about in no particular order, unless that is the correct way to read the spread. Such spreads are very complicated and usually use the entire deck, so they are beyond the scope of this book.

the nature of your reading

While you are reading the cards and discussing their meanings with the questioner, pay attention to their behaviour and body language because these will tell you whether they are comfortable with what you are saying. If your client looks distinctly uneasy or keeps shifting about in their seat, it is obvious that something is wrong. Rather than carry on regardless, gently ask them if they are okay. You may have unwittingly touched on a subject that they find very upsetting and which they might want to talk about. However, you must respect their wishes if they do not want to discuss it, especially if you are not a trained counsellor or psychotherapist. You may be straying into areas that are the emotional equivalent of dynamite and which you are unqualified to deal with. Always be tactful, and tread very carefully. It is better to be tentative than to trample all over someone's carefully constructed defences with hob-nailed boots because you want to prove to yourself that your intuition is right.

You must therefore respect a questioner's right to deny things that you are telling them. It may be obvious to you from the cards that their mother was a domineering matriarch who has almost completely crushed their spirit, but they may not agree with you, nor thank you for saying so. So if you ask something like 'Did your mother have a big influence on you?' or 'Was she a larger than life figure?' (which is always a useful euphemism for people who are difficult, bossy or domineering), and they tell you that she was the sweetest, most gentle woman they have ever known, you should not respond by saying 'Nonsense, I can see that she was an absolute bitch'. They may not yet be ready to face up to the truth, and it is essential that you accept this. Equally, you have to be open to the idea, no matter how alarming it might be, that your intuition or interpretation of the cards could be wrong.

imparting bad news

When talking to people who have never had their cards read, I often hear such comments as: 'I don't want a reading because I don't want to know if something bad is going to happen to me'; 'It scares me'; and even 'I don't want to be told when I'm going to die'. Some of your questioners may entertain such thoughts, even if they never articulate them. You therefore have a responsibility to set their minds at rest and not to scare them. If some of the more difficult cards appear in the reading, these alone may frighten the questioner so you will have to reassure them, for instance by pointing out that the Death card does not refer to a physical death but rather to psychological change.

There are times when a reading seems to be full of bad news or has very negative overtones. Your intuition may be telling you that things do not look good for your questioner, but should you say so? It is difficult to make generalisations about this because each case is different. You might decide to issue a gentle warning about something, perhaps advising the questioner to have a check-up with their doctor if their health seems to be the problem, or suggesting that they reassess their finances if these appear to be causing the most anxiety.

However, you should avoid making dire prognostications because they may be wrong, for a number of reasons. The tarot reflects the situation at the time of the reading but this can always change. Simply giving someone a gentle warning could be enough to make them take the necessary remedial action to avert disaster. You may also be reading too much into the cards and leaping to conclusions, or there is a chance that you have completely misinterpreted the spread. And there is even a possibility that the cards are wrong, as any number of external factors, from tension in the room to the questioner feeling unwell, can affect their accuracy. It is irresponsible to gloss over difficult readings and ignore their warnings, but it is also careless to fill your questioner with fear and dread. As you gain more experience with the tarot, you will find it easier to cope when you get a negative reading. Even so, it is always better to play something down than to dramatise it and alarm your questioner.

finishing the reading

At the end of the reading, ask the questioner whether they have any queries. They may want you to amplify something that you touched on earlier, or they might take this as an opportunity to reveal the real reason why they have come for a reading, especially if they have denied or hidden it up until that point. For instance, the person with the tricky mother might suddenly start admitting that she was not quite as easy as he or she would like to think. This is very similar to an experience that many doctors speak of, where their patient discusses a minor symptom and only discloses their true health problem when they are on their way out of the door. So do not be surprised if the questioner who comes to you with one problem eventually reveals that they are also struggling with something much bigger.

When the reading is over, you must once again cleanse and ground yourself. You do this in the same way that you began the reading. If you are tuned into the seven major *chakras* in your energy field, you will want to achieve mental closure and then imagine that you are encased in a bubble of white light. If the reading has been particularly difficult or the questioner has left a tense atmosphere behind them, you can cleanse the room by opening the window, smudging with some sage or using whichever technique you find most effective. It may also help to wash your hands and to bathe the tarot cards with white light. If you follow these procedures, you will protect yourself, and your questioners, from difficult energies, and your tarot readings will be more effective as a result.

the major arcana

o the fool

At its best, The Fool symbolises an act of faith; at its worst it represents foolhardiness, a tendency to rush into things without thinking them through and an inability to learn from one's mistakes. The illustration on this card shows a youth standing on a ledge, apparently completely unaware of the peril in which he has placed himself. Instead of looking at his feet to ensure he does not tumble into the abyss, his eyes are fixed in beatific gaze on the sky. He carries a rose in one hand and has slung a small pack of belongings over his other shoulder. A small dog stands by his feet, possibly ready to warn him of imminent danger or perhaps having a lovely time barking at the birds.

the innocence of youth

The Fool is not looking at his current situation because he is much more interested in what lies beyond it. This may or may not be wise. Perhaps he has checked that he is safe and so is able to enjoy the scenery without a qualm. Or maybe he is one of those foolish people who climb mountains without adequate preparation and then have to be rescued, thereby putting other people's lives in danger as well as their own.

When this card appears it often refers to the mixture of joy and fear that accompanies a new relationship. You fall in love and it feels like the first time. Yes, you may have been in love before but it was never like this. Yes, you have been hurt in the past but this relationship will last for ever. This is the real thing! You feel on top of the world, just as the Fool is apparently on top of the world. In this way, the Fool represents the innocence of youth, the ability to ignore the unhappy past and trust that the future will be so much brighter. It may also illustrate the ability to overlook the fact that you said all this last time around.

Yet the nagging doubts may be there under the surface. Are you about to make the same old mistakes all over again? Are you so busy enjoying being in love that you have failed to notice the pitfalls that can accompany this state? Or are you faintly worried that you have fallen for the wrong person and your heart will be broken? Are you waiting for a friend to act like the small dog at the Fool's heels and bark a warning at you? If they do not warn you and things do go wrong, will you somehow find a way of blaming them for not saying anything?

Alternatively, perhaps you are represented in this card by the small dog and not the Fool. Maybe you are anxious that your friend is about to take a mighty leap into the unknown and you are concerned about their welfare. Should you interfere or is it none of your business?

the wise fool

Whatever your role in the situation, it may help to remember the concept of the wise fool. In *King Lear*, the Fool protected his master even when Lear was at his most irrational and deluded. It was evident that the Fool was in complete command of his wits, unlike his master. Life is not always as black and white as we like to think. Someone who seems to be acting in a completely foolish way may turn out to be eminently wise.

I the magician

You know when you have met the person who embodies the Magician. They are skilled at using language and may even make a living from the clever use of words. They may also be heavily involved in business. They are charming, creative, original and have many talents at their disposal. They may also have a vast store of knowledge about all manner of things; the sort of person who is invaluable when you are trying to complete a crossword or general knowledge quiz. It is unlikely that they are a specialist, however, because that may require a form of effort, concentration or commitment that they are unwilling to give.

Whenever the Magician appears in a spread it is essential to be alert to the possibility of trickery. This person may seem very plausible but do they always tell the truth? Perhaps they are such good company, so well connected or so hypnotically attractive, that you are keen to give them the benefit of the doubt and will turn a deaf ear to any statements that sound hollow or strike the wrong note. Small squeaks of disquiet may arise when this person says things that do not add up, but you firmly shove them to the back of your mind.

This may be how things continue. You might always have a slight mistrust of this person even if you never fully admit it to yourself. Yet you may never have cause to regret your association with them, perhaps because you are sufficiently wary of them or because deep down you know exactly who you are dealing with and treat them accordingly.

whose fault is it anyway?

A less happy situation arises when you are duped or deceived by the person represented by the Magician. When this happens, as it frequently does, and you find you have been dropped right in it and left to cope while your Magician friend does a disappearing act, you will probably rail against them and blame them for everything that has happened. But you may also be secretly furious with yourself for allowing the problem to develop in the first place. If you are honest, you will probably realise that you knew all along that this person was unreliable or possibly even a crook. So you may tell yourself that you are partly to blame for the outcome. You will not want to admit this to anyone else, of course, because that might make you look even more foolish than you already feel. If this person has illegally taken something that belongs to you or tricked you out of some money, you may even be reluctant to report them to the appropriate authority because you do not want to lose face.

The Magician is not telling you that no one can be trusted. Nor is it suggesting that someone who is slightly shady will turn out to be a complete scoundrel. However, it is warning you to be on your guard, and also to be aware of your own ability to deceive both yourself and others. If you are considering becoming emotionally or financially involved with someone who fulfils many of the characteristics of the Magician, this card may be sounding louder alarm bells. You might not have any conscious reason to suspect them of duplicity but the possibility may still exist.

THE MAGICIAN

II the high priestess

This card is telling you to trust your intuition and to follow your gut instincts. These are much more powerful than you may imagine and they carry important messages for you. If you are able to tune into your intuition, you will gain tremendous insight and inner knowledge.

finding your inner high priestess

In ancient times, a High Priestess was an immensely powerful woman who was able to commune with the gods and dispense knowledge and advice to her fellow mortals. She was privy to some of the secrets of the universe and so was highly revered. She also had an air of mystery and seemed separate from other people. When this card appears in a spread, it indicates that you must find the High Priestess within you. Gender is not relevant here because we are dealing with an archetype, so both men and women can gain meaning from the High Priestess. You are being urged to get in touch with your own intuitive abilities and to

THE HIGH PRIESTESS

trust your instincts, no matter what they are telling you. Sometimes the messages the universe is sending you may not be very palatable or welcome and you may be tempted to ignore them in the hope that your instincts will soon tell you something more pleasant. However, life does not always work like this and occasionally we are forced to embrace darker and more difficult experiences than we would like. High Priestesses were able to enter other realms, and this card is directing you to embrace both the dark and light sides of life.

Pay extra attention to your dreams because they could have special relevance for you at the moment, especially if you are prepared to analyse them in detail. You might even want to investigate dream symbolism in order to explore them on a deeper level. If you have been wondering whether to consult a medium or someone else with psychic gifts, this card indicates that it would be a good time to do so, provided you have chosen someone who is reliable. It will be important to use your discrimination in this, so do not automatically believe everything you are told. If something does not ring true you may be completely justified in discounting it. Alternatively, of course, you might be dismissing something because you do not want to believe it. Nothing is cut and dried in the realm of the High Priestess.

If you are wondering whether to learn a new subject or embark on a period of study, especially if it has spiritual or religious overtones, this card suggests that it will be a valuable thing to do.

meeting the high priestess in others

If you think this card refers to someone else, they are powerful, wise and intuitive if not actually psychic. You may go to them for advice, perhaps because you are worried about something. They could be a teacher or mentor, so you can learn from their experience and knowledge. If you are lucky, they are objective and perceptive, and you can trust them. However, be wary of simply imagining that someone has these qualities without seeing evidence of them for yourself.

III the empress

Fertility, abundance and creativity are all described by this card. As such, it is one of the most favourable cards of the Major Arcana because it indicates a time of happiness, expansion and fruition. You can make a lot of progress, especially in areas connected with your home, family and anything else that makes you feel safe and content.

As its name suggests, the Empress can refer to a specific woman in your life, such as your partner, mother, sister, daughter, aunt or friend. She may play an especially important role at the time of the reading or you might be concerned about her welfare and be seeking reassurance that she is all right. There is a strong maternal quality to the Empress, and you may be called upon to provide this for someone else, whether you are male or female. Alternatively, this card could be suggesting that you mother yourself in some way. For instance, if life has been rather grim lately it would be a good opportunity to take greater care of your own wellbeing.

the birth of something new

The Empress is a fecund and fertile archetype, so this card could refer to a pregnancy or the birth of a child. On the other hand, it might describe the birth of an idea or project, since it represents both literal and metaphorical forms of fertility. It can therefore also indicate the need to become more connected to nature, perhaps by spending some time in beautiful surroundings outdoors, by cultivating your garden or by moving to the country. If you currently feel disconnected from life and ungrounded, contact with the earth will help you to overcome this, even if all you do is tend a window box. You will also experience happiness by doing things that give you pleasure or fulfilment.

If you have been wondering when to start a venture that you hope will bring you joy or creative satisfaction, the appearance of the Empress is a good indication that you should begin it soon. Do not delay for long because you

THE EMPRESS

may miss your opportunity or lose your inspiration. Just as there are seasons for planting crops and seasons for harvesting them, so you should choose the right time to begin new projects in order to give them the best chance of success.

forging new relationships

The Empress can indicate the beginning of a relationship that will be fulfilling or give you the chance to grow in some way as a person. If you have recently met someone and are wondering whether the situation will travel in the direction you want, this card suggests that it might. It can describe making an emotional commitment to someone, whether on a romantic or platonic level, and can be a marvellous indication of a happy partnership, such as a marriage. It can also point towards a fulfilling business relationship in which everyone will work together to create something of value and beauty.

THE EMPEROR

IV the emperor

Few people are more powerful than an emperor, so this card denotes authority, strength and influence. The Emperor may be telling you that you have more power and ability than you give yourself credit for, or you might meet these qualities through another person. If you are currently searching for a job or you want greater responsibility, this card is a good indication that you will get what you are looking for. It may also be saying that you must believe in yourself before you can expect anyone else to place their trust in you.

the ultimate authority figure

Very often, the Emperor refers to someone who is considered to be in a position of authority. This might be reflected in their career, perhaps because they are a teacher, doctor or politician, or in their spare-time activities. They have a good sense of their own importance, probably without letting it go to their head. They are more likely to have worldly than spiritual power, and they do not have to be a man. If this card represents a woman, she is respected for her achievements and she has a natural air of authority. She may be expressing the masculine and powerful side of her personality.

If the card refers to you rather than someone else, it is reminding you of your own power and influence. Perhaps you need to take control of a difficult situation rather than allow things to drag on as they are for much longer. You may have to put your foot down about something or be the one who instigates some important changes. Do not be frightened to speak up if no one else will, nor to show the steely part of your nature if you think it is necessary.

The illustration shows a man wearing a crown, holding an orb and sceptre, and whose robe is pulled back to reveal a suit of armour. This suggests that he is willing to go into battle if needs be, although he would prefer to exert his authority through more peaceful means. You may therefore want to imitate him by showing that you are also prepared to do battle over something if all else fails. This card is ruled by Aries, which is a headstrong sign and has a tendency to rush in where angels fear to tread. You will have to decide whether this is a sensible strategy or whether you should curb such impulses and be more restrained.

The Emperor is a man whose head rules his heart, so this card may be telling you to make some hard decisions in which there is no place for sentiment. In the picture, the landscape behind him is rocky and uncompromising, showing that he must deal with the nitty-gritty and be tough.

the man in your life

If this card does not describe you, it may refer to an important man in your life. This could be your partner, son, father, brother or uncle, or someone else who is very involved with you at the time of the reading. He may be rather sombre or serious, or he could be implacable about something. You might find him stern or authoritarian, yet you need his help or advice. As a result, you will not necessarily like what he says although you will recognise the wisdom of it.

V the hierophant

In some decks, this card is called the Pope, as a reminder of the spiritual depth and mystery with which it is associated. Although it can occasionally refer to a person, the Hierophant usually describes a situation in which it is best to behave in a conventional, prudent and unflamboyant manner. It does not suggest that you draw a lot of attention to yourself; instead, you should be circumspect and play by the rules.

When this card refers to a person, it is someone who has some form of spiritual authority, whether it has been conferred by a recognised body or it is simply part of their personality. They also have a good knowledge of human nature, with all its possible twists and turns, so are an excellent choice of confidant or adviser if you need some help.

THE HIEROPHANT

the search for spiritual meaning

The card shows the Hierophant holding a triple cross, which represents the ability to meld the material, physical and spiritual aspects of life. Therefore, it may be telling you to blend your religious needs with the more mundane areas of your existence. For instance, this might be a good opportunity to make sure you practise what you preach, or to set aside time each day for some form of spiritual activity, such as meditation or prayer.

If the card appears at a time when you are having difficulties with other people, it may be encouraging you to look beyond petty differences and to try to discover what draws you together. It may also be warning against a tendency to take the moral high ground or pontificate about how others should be behaving. Instead of judging them, perhaps you should concentrate on your own behaviour, especially if there is a chance that you may be doing the very thing for which you are criticising others? The Hierophant therefore stresses the qualities of compassion, understanding, tolerance, forgiveness and forbearance.

taking the conventional route

Sometimes the Hierophant counsels the need to do things in a conservative or low-key manner. It may be better to toe the traditional line than to branch out in new directions or be avant-garde. However, you must guard against the possibility of playing it so safe, that you do not take any risks at all or you become mired in outmoded ideas or lazy thinking.

placing someone on a pedestal

When the Hierophant represents a person, it carries a tacit warning not to put them on too high a pedestal. If they have a religious or spiritual authority or leadership, try not to let this cloud your opinion of them so you forget that they are human, with all the foibles that this entails. Do not make them out to be something they are not, otherwise you will be bitterly disappointed when you discover that they have feet of clay after all.

VI the lovers

This card has several meanings. It can indicate the start of a love affair or an important relationship, but it can also describe the need to make some sort of choice, such as choosing between two lovers or two jobs. In many decks, it shows a man and a woman who are looking up to a third party, which might be an angel, a cherub or a man.

love and harmony

When the Lovers describes a relationship, it is close and fulfilling. It does not necessarily have to be a love affair or marriage but it is certainly an alliance that involves deep, heartfelt sentiments and a strong emotional bond. The appearance of this card may indicate that everything is going well, and that the relationship brings you joy. Alternatively, if you have been having problems with someone, it can reassure you that everything will sort itself out in time and that you will be reconciled with each other.

If the card appears when you have just met someone to whom you are attracted and are wondering whether your relationship will develop in the way you want, it gives you plenty of encouragement.

The Lovers can describe being able to place your trust in someone and know that they will not let you down. As ever, this card carries a warning, too. It counsels against idealising your beloved to such an extent that they can do no wrong in your eyes. If this happens, you will inevitably see them in a more realistic light eventually, by which point you may feel that they have cheated you by not being the person you imagined them to be.

making a choice

The second meaning of the card is that you have to make a choice about something. Very often this involves a form of sacrifice, perhaps because you will have to renounce something that you value or love. One of the classic meanings of this card is the eternal triangle, no matter which role you are playing; this might be the case if you are involved in a clandestine relationship and have to choose between your lover and your official partner, or you could be the injured party who discovers that your partner is being unfaithful to you. Should you stay with them and forgive them, or end the relationship?

Sometimes the choice is a financial one, perhaps when you are faced with two job possibilities. One may pay well but not offer much job satisfaction, while the other one makes up for its lack of financial rewards with more creative compensations. Which should you choose? Alternatively, perhaps the dilemma is between the spiritual and materialistic, or the sacred and the secular? The presence of a third party in the card suggests that it may help to discuss your problem with someone who can help you to gain some perspective. You can bounce your ideas off them or draw on their wealth of experience. You may even wish to seek unseen guidance through prayer, or by appealing to any spiritual entities that you feel are watching over you.

VII the chariot

When something is a struggle or challenge, but is surmountable, this card offers encouragement and support, because it suggests that you will be able to rise above adversity and eventually get through this difficult time. In order to do so, you may have to use plenty of willpower and determination, with some grit thrown in for good measure. At times, you may feel as though you are out of your depth, or that you do not have the necessary tools or abilities to manage the situation, yet you will triumph in the end.

staying in control

The card shows a man driving a chariot led by two horse-like creatures, one black and one white. Yet the man has no reins, so how can he drive the chariot? The answer is that he uses his willpower and self-control, as must you when the card appears. It is very important that you keep a lid on your emotions and do not let them gallop away with you. Harness them to your best advantage, even if that means reining in your feelings or being very strict with yourself. This is no time to lose control or do things that you will later regret. You must also pay great attention to what is in front of you, just as the charioteer must watch the road ahead of him to avoid any collisions or accidents. Do not be distracted by other considerations or allow yourself to be sidetracked. Instead, focus on whatever is most important.

If there is a decision to be made, you must not rush into anything, even if it is a very tempting thought. Try to weigh up your options and possibly even let a couple of days elapse before taking action, to allow for the possibility that you will change your mind. There is a chance that you have overlooked some important details that you will only remember when you are feeling less churned up or anxious. You may also be reacting in the heat of the moment, and might therefore make decisions that will not appeal when you are feeling more temperate and calm.

THE CHARIOT

You may long to get your own back if you are angry with someone. However the Chariot warns against taking your revenge or riding roughshod over other people's feelings. This will only cause more problems than it solves, even if it brings a fleeting sense of satisfaction.

battling it out

If you are involved in a difficult relationship that is marred by arguments or violent emotions, or a normally equable partnership is going through a stressful time, the Chariot is encouraging you to stick with it. You may have to defend yourself verbally, but you will know that this is the right thing to do. Nevertheless, you must behave in ways that are fair and proper, and should resist all temptation to impose your will on others or bully them into submission. Coping with adversity does not mean making other people's lives a misery because you are feeling sorry for yourself or want them to suffer too.

VIII strength

As its name suggests, this card describes the need for strength, confidence, perseverance and courage in the face of adversity. It encourages you to dig deep within yourself to find these qualities, and to keep on fighting when a situation is hard-going. This is not always easy, of course, especially when life seems very bleak or you do not know what your next move should be, but this card implies that, in time, you will succeed.

a herculean task

The card shows a serene-looking woman prising open the jaws of a lion. You might imagine that this is foolhardy at best, if not downright suicide, but the message of this illustration is that the task ahead of you will be easier than you think. It may seem very frightening or dangerous, or require a tremendous amount of courage, but you will eventually emerge victorious.

Strength has links with the Greek myth about the labours of Hercules, who was presented with twelve tasks and who cleverly succeeded at all of them by using his wits. So this card may be telling you to keep your head when approaching the problem, and not to let yourself feel defeated by its magnitude. It may help to tackle it step by step, rather than concentrating on the end result only and wondering how you will ever manage to achieve it.

mind over matter

Some element of mind over matter may be involved in the task that lies ahead of you. The card urges strength of purpose and determination, neither of which you will achieve if you tell yourself that you are unequal to the task. So it is important to believe in yourself and in your abilities right from the start, and also to have complete confidence in a positive and successful conclusion. Some form of creative visualisation may help you in this, or you might prefer to try prayer or meditation.

For instance, if there has been a breach with someone and you are wondering how you will ever manage to heal it, this card may be telling you to focus on repairing the relationship rather than dwelling on the rift between you. It might suggest that you do this gradually, in small steps, so if you are trying not to see or think about a person, perhaps because you have broken up with them and you know it was the right thing to do, the card may be hinting that you should take it one day at a time.

knowing when to hold back

As its name implies, this card describes using strength to get through a situation, but how much should you use? Brute force, dominance or bullying may not be appropriate, even if they are tempting, because you are more likely to profit from taking a softly-softly approach.

IX the hermit

This is the card of contemplation, solitude, knowledge, caution and prudence. It speaks of the need to think things through very carefully and not to rush into decisions, perhaps because you do not yet know the whole story or because certain aspects of it have yet to come to light. It is telling you to find answers to questions that are perplexing you. The Hermit also has very strong connections with spirituality, in all its forms.

receiving divine guidance

This card shows a hooded man in a snowy landscape. He is holding up a lantern, and using its light to see the way forward. This is the key meaning of the card, because it is telling you to find something that will help you to illuminate your own path. It might be a spiritual belief, a philosophy, a religion, a myth or the pursuit of knowledge, but it is something that will shed light on your situation and guide you in the right direction.

THE HERMIT

The Hermit often appears when you are going through a difficult time or you sense that all the odds are stacked against you. You may even feel as though you are wandering through a personal wilderness because life is so bleak or lacking in comfort. You may also think you are completely on your own, with no help from any quarter. However, this card is telling you to seek guidance and succour from something numinous and bigger than yourself. This does not have to be conventional religion, but it is something that has meaning for you and which gives comfort, too. The Hermit can also refer to learning and the quest for knowledge, so can encourage you to embark on an educational project that will expand your mind and widen your understanding of the world.

the need for self-denial

The Hermit is always dressed very simply, and the card stresses the importance of self-denial. This might mean biting back those barbed comments that you long to make to someone, even though they will give you a moment's satisfaction, because they will only make the situation worse than it is already. If you are involved in an illicit relationship with someone and know that you should give them up, the Hermit may be telling you to deny your own needs or withdraw your affection for the greater good of everyone concerned. However, it carries a tacit warning not to see yourself as a martyr, nor to cast yourself in the role of saint. Both images are tricks of the ego, and you should use the Hermit's lantern as a way of becoming conscious of your motives and aware of your emotions, whatever they are.

The Hermit therefore urges you to look deep within yourself in order to know yourself better. This may involve a period of intense reflection and contemplation, perhaps accompanied by some unpleasant realisations about yourself. There is little that is comfortable about this card, and sometimes it can describe a fear of secrets coming to light. Something that you have kept in the dark may finally be exposed to the scrutiny of others.

WHEEL of FORTUNE

X wheel of fortune

Nothing in life ever stays the same. Situations are always changing, as this card reminds us. The wheel of life turns and our circumstances alter. This is the central message of the Wheel of Fortune: that life consists of change. As a result, difficult situations can become easier over time, and periods of peace and prosperity can give way to more challenging circumstances.

from bad to good

This card always offers hope if it appears when times are hard, because it suggests that the situation will alter and, hopefully, improve. The problems that you are dealing with will come to an end, or at least become more manageable in time. The nature of the surrounding cards will give you further information about this, but the Wheel of Fortune certainly indicates that change is in the air.

The illustration shows animals arranged around the wheel. As it rotates, they will move with it. This indicates that the changes in our fate, and whether we are up or down, are out of our control. Our lives may be governed by forces that are too great for us to influence. We may even be playthings of the gods, for all we know.

So, the Wheel of Fortune tells us to accept that life is never static and that we are in a constant state of flux. Therefore, we should not take anything for granted because we do not know how long it will last. When we are enjoying favourable or happy times, we should appreciate them as much as possible because we do not know when they will end. When life gets tough and we are struggling to cope with problems, we can at least content ourselves with the knowledge that they will pass in time. Meanwhile, we can learn something from the situation by paying attention to what is going on. We should live in the moment, rather than spend all our time wishing that a ghastly experience could get better, or worrying that all our happiness will evaporate and we will become miserable.

Traditionally, this card indicates that fate, or destiny, is at work. An event could alter your circumstances and you have little control over this. Your very own Wheel of Fortune will have moved on by a few notches, thus changing your situation in some way. If you were riding high, you may hit a downward turn. If you were going through a difficult phase, things could start to improve.

the end of a cycle

The Wheel of Fortune can also indicate that you have reached the end of a particular cycle or stage in your life. For instance, it might suggest the termination of a relationship and the start of a new one. This relationship may simply have reached a natural conclusion, with the wheel having turned full circle since it began.

XI justice

Justice is one of the Major Arcana cards whose title says it all. As its name implies, Justice urges fair play, the triumph of reason and the need for balanced decisions. It describes impartiality and an open mind. The illustration on this card shows a seated figure, wearing a crown to indicate authority, holding an upraised sword in one hand and a set of scales in the other. It is telling you to make decisions based on the facts and on what is fair, not on what will serve you best or will be a slap in the face for someone else.

playing fair

If you need to make a decision and Justice appears in a spread, it is urging you to behave in a reasonable and just manner and to weigh up all the pros and cons first. You may have to deliberate and take plenty of factors into account. You must be objective, dispassionate and logical. This is no time to make rash judgements or reach a verdict based entirely on your gut instincts. Instead, you must think things through carefully.

You may have to reach a compromise in the end, rather than insist on having everything on your own terms. It is also very important that you listen to other points of view, even if these are inimical to your own. You could learn something and you might even revise your own opinions once you have listened to other people. Justice warns you not to believe that you are right and everyone else is wrong until you have weighed up all the facts. Even then, you may not be in a position to judge other people.

The card also urges you not to be dogmatic about situations that you do not fully understand, since you cannot possibly appreciate what is involved. Therefore, it may be warning you against being biased, prejudiced or even bigoted, and telling you not to put people into neat pigeon-holes based on their race, gender or cultural background.

If you are involved in a legal dispute, this card brings encouraging news because it suggests that things will work

out well, provided you act in the ways it describes. For
instance, if you are in the throes of separation or divorce,
you should strive for a reasonable division of your joint
property rather than demand more than your fair share.
However, the outcome may not be so rosy if you lie, cheat or
try to trick anyone. You will be the loser, and you may also
have to face the music for your actions. Justice reminds us,
in no uncertain terms, that we get our just desserts. If we
behave well, we are rewarded, but if we misbehave we will
be chastised, pilloried or even punished.

   This card has a very pertinent message if you are locked
in a difficult situation with someone. It is telling you to rise
above your very human emotions and to do what is best for
everyone concerned. This may mean putting someone
else's welfare before your own if you think it is necessary, or
resisting the urge to get drawn into a vendetta or tit-for-tat
retaliation. It is also advising you to play by the rules,
instead of getting involved in anything underhand or sneaky.

XII the hanged man

Life is in limbo when the Hanged Man appears. You may feel as though you are in a state of suspended animation, poised between one chapter of your life and the next. Very often, you have little control over this. All you can do is wait, with as much patience as you can muster, until things begin to move again.

The Hanged Man has no connection with capital punishment or unusual forms of torture. The card depicts a man hanging from one of his feet, and his legs form the shape of the figure four. In numerology, this represents the number of matter and suggests that the Hanged Man is in a much more stable position than he looks. His halo hints that he has achieved some form of enlightenment or sanctity; this may be the wisdom to live in the present moment because that is all he has. The past has gone and the future has not yet arrived.

hanging around

It can be difficult to make much progress in any situation which is described by the Hanged Man. Instead, you may have to play a waiting game because matters are apparently out of your hands. You might be standing by for someone to make an important decision that will affect your future, such as wondering whether you will be offered a job. If a relationship is going through a stressful phase, you might be waiting for your partner to decide whether they will stay with you. You could even be expecting the results of a medical examination, such as a pregnancy test. Whatever is happening to you, the Hanged Man is telling you to live in the moment, to learn from it and to accept that you are in limbo, rather than to eagerly anticipate what will occur next or to retreat into recollections of more satisfying times.

Sometimes, this card appears when life is going through a fallow and rather dull phase. Not much is happening to you, and you may feel as though you are simply marking time until the next bout of excitement. Alternatively, the Hanged Man may indicate a much-needed respite from two very busy phases in your life, enabling you to catch your breath for a short while.

46

gaining a fresh perspective

One of the most noteworthy facts about the Hanged Man is that he is hanging upside down. This means that he has a different view of the world from the rest of us, and he is therefore urging us to see things from a different perspective as well. This might happen of its own accord when the circumstances of your life alter, perhaps as a result of radical change. You must then strive to adapt to your new situation so you can cope with it. Alternatively, the Hanged Man may be telling you that things will not improve until you can alter your attitude to them.

Sometimes the Hanged Man is urging you to renounce something. This usually involves some form of sacrifice, so it might be telling you to give up a cherished relationship because it is making both of you unhappy. Very often, there is some form of choice involved between the worldly and the spiritual or moral.

XIII death

What could be more uncompromising than this card's title? It speaks of endings, in which something has to die before something else can begin to grow. It also talks of transformation, in which subtle or dramatic alterations take place. Change is one of the central themes of the tarot, and the Death card encapsulates this. However, it rarely describes a physical death, so the card does not deserve the trepidation with which it is often greeted when it appears in a spread. Nevertheless, it suggests that fundamental changes will alter the roots of your world.

getting back to basics

Death stresses the importance of cutting back and of stripping away the old to make way for the new. The card shows a skeleton, wearing armour, riding through a bare

field. Death is telling you to clear away the dead wood in your own life so something new can grow. This may mean that compromise, or hedging your bets, is out of the question, and you have to make some radical and sweeping changes. Sometimes this will involve losing face or having to start again from scratch in a more humble position than the one you are familiar with. Although this may not be very appealing, it might be your only option and, until you accept it, you will continue to struggle against forces beyond your control or find that you are not making any progress.

This might mean ending a relationship, especially if you know that it has no more to offer you or that you have no other option. Alternatively, perhaps you do not have to make such a drastic decision, but nevertheless you must make some solid changes that will affect the partnership. For instance, you might make it clear that you will no longer tolerate someone's abuse, lies or bad behaviour.

the need for psychological change

Death often refers to a profound psychological change that is taking place. You might be going through a transitional period in which you are moving away from the person you once were, perhaps because you are becoming more aware of yourself and of your motives. You may feel as though you are growing up at last, or becoming less dependent on your family and more able to stand on your own two feet. If you have been locked in a particular pattern of behaviour, you may now find the key that helps you to escape from it or at least to realise what has been happening. You might even think about going to see a therapist or counsellor so you can talk through your difficulties.

Whatever you decide to do, or whatever happens to you, this card is telling you that the experience will have a profound and long-lasting effect. When you look back on this period in your life, you may feel that it was necessary because it taught you something valuable about yourself and enabled you to draw on strengths that perhaps you did not know you had.

XIV temperance

Temperance urges moderation in all things. It warns against overdoing anything, stepping out of line or being separated from whatever nourishes you. Instead, Temperance says, you must be frugal, self-controlled and careful. You must also achieve some form of harmony so you can successfully blend various areas of your life, or find a way to balance your material and spiritual needs.

holding back

When this card appears in a spread it is telling you to make some adjustments to your life. You may be overworking so you need to slow down. You could be caught up in a painful relationship that robs you of your self-respect, and which you need to end as soon as possible. You might be spending too much money and have to cut back on your expenses. Your health could be suffering because you are

50

burning the candle at both ends or drinking too much, so you need to be kinder to yourself or more abstemious. You could be heaping coals of fire on your head because you did something that you consider to be wrong, in which case perhaps you need to stop blaming yourself and also to ask for forgiveness from the other person.

Although this card depicts an angel pouring a liquid from one goblet to another, Temperance is not telling you to become a saint. It is not suggesting that you wear a hair shirt or become holier-than-thou. In fact, it is warning against such forms of behaviour because these are just as extreme as being drunk or exhausted from overwork, for example. Rather, it is telling you to exercise moderation, compromise and patience.

achieving a balance

Temperance talks of the importance of achieving some form of balance in your life. Very often, this means finding ways to blend the spiritual and secular elements of your existence so they work together and you become a more rounded individual as a result. If you have been neglecting your spiritual nourishment while concentrating on materialistic concerns, this might be a good time to redress the balance. Conversely, if you spend most of your time thinking about other realms or are busy with a devotional practice, and are out of touch with the rest of your life, you need to become more grounded and practical.

a good example

Sometimes, this card describes someone who will be a good influence or a shining example to you. They may be a friend who helps you through a bad patch or someone who acts as a mentor or counsellor. Alternatively, you might fulfil this role for someone who needs your advice, your support or your sponsorship. If you find yourself cast in this role, take note of Temperance's warning against thinking of yourself as a saint or martyr because then you will need to find your own sense of balance before you can help others.

XV the devil

One of the most maligned and misunderstood cards in the tarot, the Devil describes a sense of enslavement or bondage to someone or something. There is a feeling of being trapped in a situation and unable to break free, although that may not be the reality. The problem may seem too huge to struggle with or solve, or your mind may skitter away from it in fear every time you begin to think about it. As a result, it feels like a massive blight on your life and the bane of your existence.

The Devil has no links with black magic, voodoo, witchcraft or possession. Its appearance in a spread does not mean that someone will put the evil eye on you, or that the devil is hiding in the shadows waiting to grab your soul. Occasionally, it can mean that someone is being spiteful or malevolent, or they are setting you a bad example.

addiction and subjugation

This card often describes some form of addiction from which it is very hard to break loose. This could be something that is generally recognised to cause problems, such as an addiction to nicotine, alcohol, narcotics, food, sex, violence or gambling. There are support groups and other sources of help for anyone wanting to give up one of these habits, although the addict may feel unable even to contemplate such a move because it seems beyond them. However, the message of the Devil is that mastering the problem may be very difficult but it is by no means impossible.

Of course, there are many other addictions to which we are all prey and which operate in more subtle ways. You might be drawn to relationships in which you are always cast in a subservient role or you subjugate your needs to those of your partner. You could be so used to thinking 'poor me', and basking in other people's sympathy, that you do not know how to break out of this attitude and assert yourself. If so, this card is telling you that you need to become more aware of what is going on so you can do something constructive about it.

THE DEVIL

breaking the chains

This card shows a huge, winged devil looming over a naked man and woman. They both have chains wrapped loosely around their necks, yet it is obvious that they could easily slip these off and run away. So why have they not done so? This is the crux of the message that the Devil contains, and it is not always an easy question to answer. If you feel trapped in a dead-end job from which you long to escape, you may decide that it is better to stay put because at least you know what you are dealing with. Better the devil you know, you tell yourself. If you are estranged from someone and unhappy about it, you may be adamant that you will not make the first move because the whole situation is the other person's fault and it is up to them to apologise first. However, the Devil is reminding you to examine your own role in what has happened and to break free from the imprisonment of your self-defeating attitudes.

XVI the tower

The events foretold by this card are radical, shocking and often unexpected. You may feel as though you have been hit by a bolt from the blue, with trouble apparently coming out of nowhere. This can lead to dramatic changes which often involve embarrassment, a loss of prestige or a reversal of fortune. When you look back on the situation, you may realise that problems had been brewing for a long time but you had failed to notice them, or had hoped that they would resolve themselves without any action on your part.

Sometimes this card describes a loss of income and status, so you have to start again. For instance, it can sometimes indicate bankruptcy. Although this is naturally very disturbing and worrying at the time, when the dust has settled you may realise there are benefits to what has happened. You might have reordered your life in a way that you find more satisfying than before. There is even a

THE TOWER

possibility of feeling relieved that the axe has finally fallen because it has ended the sense of dread that you felt at the thought of what might go wrong.

all is not lost

The image on this card is dramatic, showing a couple falling to the ground from the top of a tower. A bolt of lightning has struck the tower, knocking off its roof in the way one slices off the top of a boiled egg. The people tumbling to the ground look shocked but one imagines that they will not be killed in the fall. They are certainly not injured from the lightning strike on the tower. This is a reassurance that although the changes described by the Tower will mean you have to reorganise your life, sometimes in quite radical ways, you will survive what happens. Nevertheless, the experience will not be easy or pleasant and it may take some time to recover from it, both materially and emotionally.

unpleasant revelations

Since this card describes loss of face, it can mean that you will be embarrassed by what happens in a relationship. You might discover that your partner has been unfaithful, and that you were apparently the last to know. Someone might let you down in a very public fashion, so you not only have to cope with the disappointment but also the fact that your fate is common knowledge. You might have to revise your opinion of someone in the light of their behaviour, much to your chagrin. Alternatively, of course, you may be the one who is caught out and who has to face the music. If so, you can expect this music to be rather loud.

Another way to interpret the Tower is to see it as a high pedestal from which someone has fallen. Perhaps you have been too idealistic about a partner and must now realise that they are only human after all? Or maybe you have given the impression that you are something you are not, and must now accept that other people are angry that you have deceived them or made fools of them. You must now have the courage to show who you really are, warts and all.

XVII the star

This is one of the most positive and heartening cards in the entire tarot. It is the wish card of the Major Arcana, and as such always gives encouraging news that difficult situations will improve and, sometimes, that dreams will come true. If you have been struggling with an intransigent problem, the Star offers you hope and reassurance, and encourages you to believe that everything will come right in the end. It is especially welcome when it appears in a spread littered with difficult cards, because it tends to ameliorate their meanings and tells you that things may not be as bad as you fear.

on the up

If life has been difficult for you, perhaps because you have been coping with an illness, a dead-end job or a stressful relationship, the appearance of the Star tells you that the situation is improving and will continue to get better. Life is on the up once more. However, this may not happen of its own accord and without any input from you. For instance, you may not get very far if you simply sit back and wait for better times to arrive by themselves. You have to get the ball rolling, perhaps by actively looking for another job or by instigating a heart-to-heart conversation with your partner. Nevertheless, if you are prepared to help yourself in some way you can rest assured that your prospects are improving.

a spiritual being

Bright stars have often been taken to foretell the birth of a spiritual master, and this card may be encouraging you to take a more spiritual approach through life. This is especially important if you have been concentrating on more mundane or material matters and feel that something central is missing from your existence. In this regard, the Star has a similar message to Temperance, because it is urging you to find a balance between the different areas of your life, and to combine them in ways that will be fulfilling and nourishing. Yet it is not telling you to concentrate on the

spiritual and numinous to the detriment of your daily life.
That would be just as unbalanced as denying your spiritual
needs while focusing intently on your physical and material
desires. Instead, as so many mystics have taught, you
should remember that you are not a human being on a
spiritual path but a spiritual being living on the human plane.
You must acknowledge both the human and otherworldly
qualities within you. The Star reminds you that there are
many ways to do this, whether you choose to belong to an
organised religion or seek the Divine through less formal
routes. The card has a particular affinity with astrology, and
this might be one area of interest for you to explore.

The Star also urges you to find a balance between other
areas of your life, such as fulfilling your work commitments
while also paying attention to your family's needs, or enjoying
an active social life while taking care of your health. In addition,
it encourages you to take a less polarised view of society, for
instance by being more accepting of people as they truly are,
without mentally putting them into 'good' and 'bad' categories.

XVIII the moon

Nothing is quite as it seems with the Moon. The key to this card is that moonlight plays tricks on us because it alters the appearance and colour of landscapes, so we are not entirely sure what we are looking at. When the Moon appears in a spread it is telling you that, for some reason, you are not seeing a situation in its true light. This might be because you are reluctant to face unpleasant facts or because someone is holding things back from you. Whatever the circumstances, you should be on your guard and do your best to be aware of what is going on, however difficult this may be.

deception and self-deception

The Moon is a difficult card because it shows that a situation is confused and murky. Nothing is clear-cut and you feel as though you are in a fog. People are not being straight with you, either. For instance, someone will say one thing and do

THE MOON

the complete opposite, so you do not know where you stand. You may even doubt that you have understood them correctly, so you begin to wonder whether you have misinterpreted their words or actions. What is more, you could become unsure of your own motives and goals.

It is hard to know whether others are deceiving you or you are fooling yourself about them. If someone keeps letting you down and coming up with what sound to you like lame excuses, should you believe them or challenge them to tell you the truth? Besides, how will you know the truth when you hear it? You may have already heard it and dismissed it, perhaps because you did not like it or it did not match your view of the situation.

Of course, you might not always be the innocent party, and you may be the one who is deliberately trying to confuse someone else or pull the wool over their eyes. If so, the Moon is warning you that you are playing a dangerous game because it is highly likely that your deception will come to light.

listening to the unconscious

This card has strong links with dreams and the unconscious, both of which can play tricks on you when it appears in a spread. Secrets or fears that you have been trying to push to the back of your mind may start to emerge unbidden, forcing you to acknowledge them. However, if this happens you should consider that you may be deluding yourself in some way. For instance, you might be plagued by a disturbing memory which is a distortion of what really happened, yet you will not know it at the time. One extreme example of this is false memory syndrome, in which someone starts to 'remember' something that never happened, but which can cause tremendous pain or division in their relationships.

On the other hand, your unconscious may also help you, perhaps by making your intuition more active or giving you a vivid dream life. If you are able to filter the messages your unconscious is giving you under the influence of the Moon, you will find that it is very helpful.

59

XIX the sun

This is one of the most joyful and positive cards in the entire tarot deck. It represents love, generosity of heart, creativity, affection and spontaneity: qualities that enrich us when we meet them in other people and also when we express them ourselves. The Sun can also describe the birth of something enjoyable, whether it is a child, a new relationship, a marriage or a project that will offer us exciting opportunities.

life-enhancing energy

The sun is the centre of our solar system and is vital for the continuation of life on this planet. When the sun's heat, light and energy eventually fizzle out, our planet will cease to be a source of life and become an inert lump of rock spinning through the darkness. In the same way, the Sun is a card that carries life-enhancing energy and love, brightening up any spread it graces. When it represents someone in your life, it shows that they bring you happiness, contentment and warmth. If they were to disappear, it would feel as though a light had been switched off. The Sun describes love, which is essential for our survival.

holding on for dear life

This card contains a warning, as does each of the tarot cards. While representing love, which is arguably the most important element in our lives and the most powerful force in the universe, and encouraging us to rejoice in it, the Sun warns against developing such a childlike, emotional dependency on the people around us that we feel our very survival will be threatened if they leave us.

If you are currently facing the prospect of the end of a relationship and this card appears, you need to ask yourself some tough questions. Are you guiltily relieved that the relationship is coming to an end? Perhaps the metaphorical sun comes out for you at the very thought of no longer having to see a certain person? Or is the reverse true? Are

THE SUN

you reacting to the imminent loss as though you are a small child about to be deprived of both its parents? In astrology, the sun represents our sense of identity, so you may feel that your own identity will vanish when you no longer have a particular person to reflect it back to you. Yet if you view this situation dispassionately and honestly, you will realise that, unless you are physically incapable of looking after yourself, your bodily survival is not literally threatened by the loss of someone dear to you.

a celebration of life

If you draw this card at a difficult time in your life, it brings you the gift of hope and the promise of better things to come. If you have encountered problems in a relationship, these may be resolved with time and love. The card also reminds you to stay positive. It may help to reflect on the Zen Buddhist concept that the sun continues to shine even when it is obscured by cloud. So life is still to be enjoyed, and you can still experience happiness, even when things are very tough.

XX judgement

This card has a very simple meaning, because it talks of the need to forgive others and the importance of acknowledging that they may also have to forgive you for something. It describes the ability to offer someone a second chance if they have transgressed in some way, even if this is difficult. There may also be a need to assess the part you have played in certain situations, especially if you feel that you have not handled these as well as you might.

the trumpet shall sound

The card depicts an angel sounding a trumpet, while bodies rise up from graves. They are gazing at the sky and holding out their arms in supplication. This image underlines the simple message of this card: that you are either being judged or in a position to judge others.

If you are being judged, you may be wishing that you had acted differently in some way. You might have incurred legal problems, be in conflict with someone or you could be having a difficult time with a partner. Maybe you are having sleepless nights over the consequence of your actions, and find yourself endlessly thinking about the problems that you have incurred? There is also a chance that you are secretly feeling hard-done-by because of what has happened, perhaps telling yourself that it is not really all your fault. When this happens, it is easy to get caught up in self-justification as a way of escaping some uncomfortable facts about yourself. You may find that the simplest option is to say sorry, and to mean it.

If you are in a position to judge other people, you should be very careful. Most of us have a tendency to make judgements about others, often without any understanding of what they are going through. Many spiritual teachings warn against judging others and speak of the need to pay attention to our own behaviour rather than that of anyone else. Yet, of course, this can be so difficult. We are often full of excuses for our own lapses while being full of anger about those of others. This card may therefore be telling you that this attitude is unhelpful and that you must rise above it by finding it in your heart to truly forgive someone for what they have done. You do not have to forget it, and there may even be reasons why it would be unwise to do so, but you must do your best to overlook what has happened or at least to stop it dominating your life.

rebirth

Judgement also speaks of rebirth and rejuvenation. If a relationship has been in the doldrums but you would like to revive it, this card is encouraging you to do so. It suggests that there is a good chance you will be successful and that your relationship will enter a new phase as a result. Yet Judgement can speak of other forms of rebirth as well, such as the transition from depression to a more up-beat and optimistic attitude, or the need to give yourself a second chance if you have been castigating yourself about something.

JUDGEMENT

XXI the world

This is the last card of the Major Arcana, so it carries a
sense of achievement and culmination. The wheel of the
Major Arcana has come full circle. Something has been
attained and we are ready to move on to new beginnings.
Therefore, this card talks of completion and success, and
the satisfaction of knowing that a job has been well done.

The World is also one of the tarot cards that speaks of
change. Sometimes, it signifies radical reform, such as the
uprooting that is involved when you move from one country
to another, or when you switch careers or partners. As its
name implies, it can be associated with travel, so it may
indicate that major changes will take place as the result of a
journey. You might have a holiday that completely alters your

attitude about something that you consider to be important, or you might have a life-changing encounter while you are travelling. Of course, this journey may be mental instead of physical, such as a course of education or a quest for spiritual wisdom.

worldly success

Sometimes, this card describes worldly accomplishments and success. These might be attained through your career or by achieving a particular goal as a result of your hard work and determination. However, after the excitement has died down you may be left wondering what you are going to do next, and you could feel a slight sense of anticlimax. 'Now what?' you may ask yourself, or you might be tempted to rest on your laurels and not do anything else for a while. This will be fine for a short period but then, the World tells you, it would be advisable to set yourself some new goals and to start to work towards them.

the world is your oyster

This is a very positive card because it carries such a strong sense of promise and ability. If you have been going through a difficult period, it is indicating that there is still much to hope for and there are many things to play for. You should not restrict yourself unduly, nor tell yourself that there is no point in even attempting to achieve something because you will never manage it. Instead, the World is encouraging you to give it your best shot and to have faith in yourself.

When this card appears in a spread, you may find that you become more interested in global affairs. For instance, you might want to know more about another country, perhaps because you plan to visit it or simply because it intrigues you. You might even become involved with someone who comes from another part of the world, whether you know them as a friend, colleague or lover. Find out all you can about the world in which you live and learn to guard against filing people into convenient pigeon-holes or assuming that someone fits into a cultural stereotype.

the minor arcana
wands

ACE of WANDS

ace of wands

Aces always rule the birth of something, and the Ace of Wands governs the start of an enterprise that will capture your imagination and create a great deal of excitement. It may be something that gives you a new lease of life after a rather dull and lacklustre phase, and it will offer you all sorts of interesting opportunities. Life is about to become much more lively and stimulating when the Ace of Wands appears.

travel broadens the mind

Wands rule all forms of travel, whether mental or physical, so the Ace of Wands can describe the start of an interesting journey. If it is a physical journey, such as a holiday or long-distance trip, it will be enjoyable and will give you plenty to think about. It may teach you something very valuable, perhaps about yourself or about the place you are visiting. It could be quite eventful or involve a challenge. You may even find that it stimulates your interest in life and fills you with a longing for pastures new. This is especially likely if you are feeling drained at the time of the reading and need to be revitalised.

If you are about to embark on a mental journey, perhaps by beginning to study a subject that interests you, it will enrich your life in some way. It could also lead you in directions that you do not anticipate at this stage, possibly even developing into a fascinating interest. This will be confirmed if the card is accompanied by the Ace of Swords.

taking a chance

Sometimes the Ace of Wands rules the beginning of a challenge or speculative venture that will be very exciting. It could tax your ingenuity in some way or provide a platform for some of your talents. Even though it may not always be plain sailing, you will enjoy putting yourself to the test and seeing if you can measure up to what is expected of you. There is even a possibility that you will be carried away by excitement once the project has got off the ground, and that you will be swept along by the momentum of it.

a change of vision

If your prospects for the future have seemed rather predictable or uninspiring, the Ace of Wands can herald a change. Your vision of the future may alter as new possibilities dawn on you. You might even be inspired to revise some of your hopes and wishes for the future, perhaps discarding certain plans and choosing others that are far more interesting and challenging. Look in the spread for other cards that describe change, such as the World, the Wheel of Fortune, Death, the Fool or any of the other Aces. If you have been bogged down in a rut, or unable to look beyond the mundane practicalities of life, your attitude will soon improve and your horizons will begin to open up, offering you new prospects and opportunities. This is not something to be sniffed at, so make the most of it.

67

two of wands

This card is encouraging you to assess your current position, especially in the light of what you have accomplished to date and what you still want to achieve. It is a particularly relevant card if you are in the early stages of a new venture or enterprise and you want to assess the progress you have made so far. You may still have a long way to go but, unless the surrounding cards tell another story, all the signs point to success and you can be reassured that you have made a good start.

Nevertheless, you should not be complacent, nor assume that everything will go well without any effort on your part. Instead, you should be vigilant about checking that you have not overlooked any essential details, and also making sure that you are in control of what is going on.

partnerships

The Two of Wands is especially favourable if you have recently become involved in a working partnership with one or more people, or you are about to take part in some negotiations. It suggests that the balance of power will be evenly spread and everyone will be happy with what develops. You may all benefit in some way, so no one loses from the arrangement and feels resentful as a result.

This is also a desirable card if you are in the process of hatching a plan or scheme with someone. Your ideas may only be pie in the sky at this point, but they are exciting and you will want to make every effort to turn them into reality. Nevertheless, they are only tentative at this stage and so they will need plenty of nourishment and enthusiasm if they are to develop into something worthwhile. You may have to take care of them as though they were young plants that are vulnerable to frost and dehydration, and which need to be nurtured.

Sometimes, the Two of Wands indicates the arrival in your life of someone you will learn from and who you can respect. They may have a rather powerful or even overwhelming personality, so you might not want to spend too much time with them. They might also have some form of professional or spiritual authority that is a strong part of their persona.

an opportunity beckons

This card can also show that an opportunity is coming your way, even though at this stage you may not know what it is. Keep your options and your mind open, so you will not miss this chance when it arrives. It may be connected with some form of personal expansion or self-development, such as travel, education or spirituality. Alternatively, you could become involved with someone who comes from another country or a completely different walk of life from your own.

three of wands

This is a positive and cheerful card, suggesting that you have embarked on a very productive and fruitful period in your life and that your enterprise, vision and creativity will bring exciting results. You are on the right track and the projects you have already started are going well. Your initial anxiety about them has passed and you now feel much more optimistic. Some of these projects have now reached the end of their initial stage and you are ready to take them one step further. There is still plenty for you to accomplish but you have made an excellent start. Later on, you may realise that this was the beginning of a tremendously successful venture, and possibly even one that proved to be a turning point for you.

If you are considering expanding a particular area of your life, such as branching out in new directions in your career, the Three of Wands is encouraging you to do so and you have good reason to feel optimistic about your chances of success.

keeping in touch

If you are currently working on plans, it may be helpful to ask other people for their opinions, even if you are pretty sure of what you want to accomplish. You could get some useful feedback from them, and they might also be able to suggest ideas that had not occurred to you. If you are working in partnership with someone, the Three of Wands is reminding you of the importance of taking this person into your confidence and sharing your ideas with them.

All the Wands are connected with travel and global concerns, and the Three of Wands has connections with international communications. You might glean some important information from someone who lives abroad, or you could be involved in a venture that includes people from other countries. It is an especially favourable card if you are taking part in some form of international trade or business.

patience

The illustration on this card shows a man standing on a hilltop, watching three ships sailing away from him. His lofty position above the water indicates that he has a good vantage point for seeing what is going on around him. The three ships represent the projects he has launched. He has done his best to ensure that they get a good start and now all he can do is to wait for them to return, bearing fruit. This will not happen overnight, and so the Three of Wands is urging you to be patient and to allow everything to develop at its own pace.

turning dreams into reality

If you have a cherished dream or vision that you want to turn into reality, the Three of Wands is encouraging you to do so. Furthermore, it suggests that you have the confidence, initiative, enterprise and enthusiasm that are needed to see it through and to make a success of it.

four of wands

The Four of Wands is telling you that it is time for a relaxing break from all your efforts. You have been working very hard and you now deserve a short rest before continuing where you left off. You are sufficiently confident about what you have achieved so far that you are able to do this with a clear conscience. This card can therefore represent a much-needed holiday, during which you will be able to unwind and pick up some of the other threads in your life that you may have had to ignore recently.

Sometimes, the Four of Wands describes the satisfaction and sense of achievement that follows the successful completion of a business project. You may have pulled off a coup of which you feel justifiably proud and which you now want to celebrate. Alternatively, you could have completed a lucrative negotiation or transaction.

enjoyment of life

This card often appears when you are emerging from a stressful period in your life, perhaps because you have been working round the clock in order to meet a deadline or fulfil a demanding schedule. You may have had to put your social life on hold but you are now ready to make contact with friends again. You are keen to enjoy life once more, especially if that means being with kindred spirits.

You will also appreciate a period of harmony with others, in which any long-running conflicts seem to fall away or become less obvious than usual. For instance, petty differences that normally arise between you and a partner may be forgotten now as you rediscover joy and pleasure in one another's company. If you are attending a gathering in which you will be seeing someone who is not exactly your first choice of companion on a desert island, it will be much easier to tolerate them than usual and you may even find to your surprise that you enjoy spending limited amounts of time with them.

emotional security

One of the most encouraging aspects of the Four of Wands is the emotional security and warmth that it promises. If the card appears when you have been going through a difficult time, it suggests that life will soon become much easier. It is a classic indication of a successful house move, especially if you will be moving to somewhere in the countryside or with a beautiful garden. This theme will be emphasised if the card is accompanied by the Empress, the Nine of Pentacles or the Ten of Cups.

If you are not considering moving house, the Four of Wands may be encouraging you to make some improvements to your existing home. The scale of these will depend on your budget, of course, but even modest improvements will increase your enjoyment of your home. They will also foster the feeling of putting down roots that will grow over time and give you a sense of belonging.

five of wands

Not an easy card, the Five of Wands describes one of those annoying phases in life when nothing goes according to plan. Arrangements that you made may have to be put on hold for the time being because of problems that are beyond your control. You may have to cope with a succession of petty disputes with people, especially if you have a working relationship with them. For instance, you might fall out with a colleague or fail to see eye-to-eye with a superior. Travel arrangements could also cause headaches now.

Some element of competition may be involved as well. You could feel that you have to jockey for position with other people in order to establish a foothold or to assert your individuality. Life may feel like one long struggle.

be patient!

This is a stage in life when you have to draw on your reserves of patience in order to cope with what is happening to you. If nothing is going right, all you can do is grit your teeth and deal with the situation. The surrounding cards will give you more information about what is going on and why. You will need to develop strength of mind and a resolute belief that everything will eventually sort itself out. Yet in the meantime you will have to be flexible when necessary, since holding your ground in some situations might make matters worse. At other times, you might be convinced that you have to stand by what you believe in, even if it makes you unpopular.

Sometimes the Five of Wands describes a deep sense of disappointment that things have not worked out in the way you anticipated. Some of your desires have been thwarted, and you feel cheated. You might be irritated because it seems as though certain people have let you down or not kept their side of the bargain. Someone that you thought was a possible collaborator may turn out to be less than inspiring, so you conclude that you are better off working by yourself. Alternatively, you could be dismayed to discover that although you thought you were embarking on an equal partnership, the other person obviously sees it as a competition in which they want to be top dog. In all such cases, you need to ask yourself whether your expectations were realistic or whether you were being far too optimistic. You might even have ignored this person's poor track record in the past, telling yourself that things would be different this time. You may also be acting competitively without realising it.

If you have been involved in a complicated venture but have neglected to keep tabs on all the small details, you might now be dealing with the irritating results. You may be meeting plenty of obstacles to your progress, or need to sort out official agreements that should have been completed a long time ago.

Travel plans could also be affected by this card, and again it is reminding you to pay attention to the small print and to crucial details. Do not trust to luck or make assumptions that are founded on nothing more than wishful thinking. You should also double-check such vital facts as whether your passport is still valid or you have adequate travel insurance.

six of wands

This is a card of achievement and triumph. Your hard work has paid off and you are currently in the happy position of being fêted for all your efforts. For a short while, you can afford to bask in the limelight and receive everyone's congratulations and acclaim. However, this is only a temporary phase and you will soon have to carry on where you left off. In the meantime, you are fully justified in feeling proud of yourself and what you have accomplished. This is a very enjoyable moment and you should make the most of it.

to the victor the spoils

The Six of Wands is a particularly welcome card if you are emerging from a gruelling phase in your life. You might have been struggling to make your way in your career, perhaps battling against competition from other people or simply trying to get yourself noticed. You have finally succeeded and can afford to rest on your laurels for a brief spell, especially if the card is accompanied by the Star, the Wheel of Fortune, Justice or the Emperor. If you were competing with other people, you can afford to be magnanimous in victory. This may also help to consolidate your position and win you everyone's support for the future.

This card can also indicate the successful conclusion to a tricky negotiation or deal, especially if it was one in which you had to rely on your wits and choose your words carefully. You may even have triumphed against the odds in some way. Wands are connected with the clever use of words and imagination, so the card could describe the successful publication of a book, poem or article. If so, this is likely to be highly original and clever. It might also indicate a successful property deal, perhaps in which you have defeated the opposition or made a fat profit.

If the Six of Wands refers to success in your career, it could be accompanied by a promotion, pay rise or fantastic new job. You may have finally reached a pinnacle of achievement, possibly putting you in the public eye and really getting you noticed. The card can also describe the attainment of a qualification or skill, such as passing an exam, gaining a university degree or passing your driving test. Naturally, the exhilaration and joy that accompany such success do not last for ever and you will soon have new projects and goals to work towards. But in the meantime you may want to pop a few champagne corks in celebration.

the leader of a team

The card shows a man wearing a laurel crown. He is on horseback, and another laurel crown is tied to the staff he carries. He is surrounded by people who are cheering him on. The Six of Wands can therefore refer to being the leader of a successful team. If this is so, you must take your share of the credit but you should make sure that you allow everyone who participated to feel that theirs was a valuable contribution as well.

seven of wands

You have come a long way and have achieved a great deal, but you are now facing a struggle or obstacle that will put you to the test. This may be in the form of competition from other people who want to oust you from your powerful position and occupy it themselves. You will have to fend them off while proving that you are capable of retaining your current position and that you can do what is expected of you.

Sometimes the Seven of Wands describes the almost inevitable difficulties that come when you have a new job or have been promoted. The time for celebration has passed and you must now prove that you are up to the task that you have been given. Will you succeed or will you be overwhelmed and have to give up? It is highly likely that success will eventually be yours, unless the surrounding cards tell a very different story. Although you cannot take this success for granted, you should have faith in yourself and your abilities.

an inner battle

The illustration for the Seven of Wands shows a young man standing on a high piece of ground. He is using his Wand to protect himself against six wands that come up to his waist. On the face of it, he seems to be in a good position, although we do not know what lies behind him and he may be in danger of falling off the edge of the elevated ground. Is he standing on the edge of a cliff or is it only a small hill?

The uncertainty surrounding his physical position mirrors the unease you are experiencing. You may feel as though you are in greater danger than is really the case, or you might be feeling much more defensive than is strictly necessary. It is difficult to know where you stand at this point, and even more so if this card is accompanied by the Moon, which will cloud your judgement still further.

Very often, the struggle depicted by the Seven of Wands takes place inside you. You may feel the burden of other people's expectations weighing heavily on your shoulders, making you worried about appearing to let yourself down or not performing at your best. You might imagine that others are snapping at your heels, longing to eject you from your position of power and occupy it themselves. Such thoughts can conjure up a pantheon of inner demons that undermine your confidence and fill you with self-doubt. Can you measure up to the competition or are you an impostor who will soon be caught out?

so near and yet so far

This card can describe a situation in which you have already achieved a great deal but you still have some way to go. You may even know that the end is in sight but nevertheless it is a struggle to muster the necessary energy for that final effort. Yet can you really give up now, when success is so close to hand?

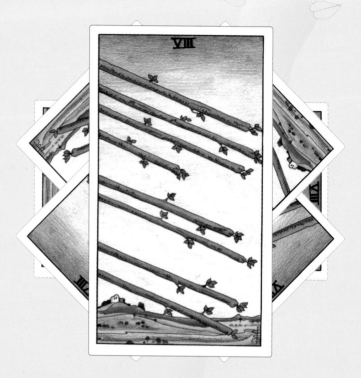

eight of wands

There is a lot going on when this card appears in a spread.
It shows that events are unfolding very quickly, sometimes
faster than you can cope with them. Projects that had been
blocked or postponed could suddenly get the go-ahead
again, filling you with a sense of urgency. Life is exciting and
there is plenty to keep you occupied. Travel is often
indicated by the Eight of Wands, especially if it is slightly
chaotic or everything has to be organised at the last minute.
The card can also describe hastily made decisions, which
may or may not work out well.

keeping busy

There is never a dull moment with this card. Any delays or
frustrations that have been holding you back are now over,
much to your relief. Life is full of promise and anticipation,
and you are raring to go again. This can be a heady

experience, especially if there is a lot that you want to achieve. You may believe that you can accomplish almost anything that you set your mind to now, and your sheer enthusiasm, initiative and energy will go a long way towards making this happen.

However, you should guard against rushing headlong into activities or decisions without carefully thinking them through first. It will be tempting to assume that everything will go according to plan as a matter of course, but this might not be the case. Remember the proverb about fools rushing in where angels fear to tread, especially if this card is accompanied by the Fool or the Knight of Swords. You should not hold back entirely but it would certainly be advisable to check your plans for potential problems or any details that you have overlooked. The nearby presence of the Five of Wands will sound an additional warning about this.

This is certainly a very exciting phase and you will undoubtedly want to make the most of it. You are blessed with additional energy and are looking for suitable outlets for it. These may include new projects and interests that you have never considered before, because at the moment you have the enthusiasm and optimism to give them a try. You will not worry about failure; what is important to you now is to broaden your horizons in every possible direction and through a wide variety of activities. Physical, mental and spiritual pursuits will all appeal, and you will enjoy the sense of not knowing where they might lead. You are filled with delicious anticipation.

travel plans

Travel is one of the classic meanings of the Eight of Wands, especially if you will be visiting a country for the first time or embarking on an adventure. Everything may happen in a rush, but that will only add to the excitement and the feeling that you do not have time to think because events are taking place so quickly. For example, you may decide to go on holiday at the last minute, or you could have to take off on a business trip at a moment's notice. It will be good fun.

nine of wands

It is not a good time to try to make progress, to expand or to
run any sort of risk. Instead, you should consolidate your
current position and bide your time until the circumstances
are more favourable.

This card can appear when you are experiencing a
temporary lull in an on-going struggle. You have a chance
to catch your breath and recharge your batteries before
having to re-enter the fray. Make the most of this
opportunity to regroup and to prepare for the next round of
difficulties. It will also be important to believe in yourself,
although this may not be easy. If you habitually put yourself
down or tell yourself that you are not nearly as capable as
everyone else you know, you will make life especially hard
for yourself now.

Sometimes, the Nine of Wands shows that problems
are just around the corner. You may want to prepare for a

difficult time by reducing your mental, physical or financial expenditure. Alternatively, you might be anticipating problems that will never happen, especially if you are aware of the threat posed by someone or something. You will have to tread a very thin line between being aware of possible problems and scaring yourself with fantasies of disaster – which is a trap you could fall into if the Nine of Swords is also near by.

finding your inner strength

No matter whether your problems are real or imaginary, whether they have already arrived or they are in the future, the Nine of Wands is encouraging you to draw on your inner reserves of strength, purpose and self-belief. Perhaps you feel exhausted by previous skirmishes or problems and are wondering how on earth you will cope with the next round of trouble. Do not worry because this card is reassuring you that not only will you manage, you will eventually succeed, especially if the Star or the Six of Wands is also in the spread. Somehow, you will find the necessary courage and strength to see things through, and to emerge victorious. It might help to rely on others for their emotional support when necessary, and it may also be sensible to take extra care of your health.

fostering your self-belief

When this card appears, it suggests very strongly that you do not have enough faith in your own abilities. Even if this is a temporary state of affairs, such a lack of confidence can be seriously undermining. It might help to remind yourself of everything you have achieved in the past, and also to make a conscious effort to block any pessimistic thoughts that cross your mind. Techniques such as creative visualisation may enable you to imagine a positive outcome to your problems. It might also be beneficial to discuss your fears and doubts with someone who is sympathetic but encouraging, and who can help you to develop a greater belief in your own abilities.

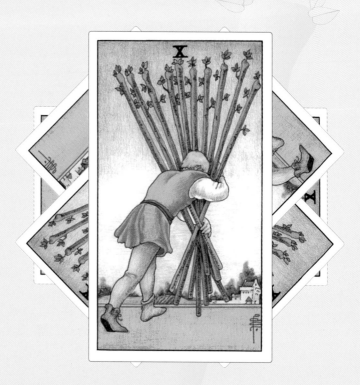

ten of wands

This card normally indicates that you are struggling with something that feels like a massive burden and which threatens to overwhelm you if you are not careful. You may have taken on more than you can cope with, such as a highly demanding job, an almost impossible goal or a negotiation in which you feel out of your depth. The question is whether life has to be so difficult. Perhaps you could ask someone for help, or maybe it would be better to lower your expectations?

taking on too much

The suit of Wands rules all forms of speculative and innovative ventures, in addition to projects that rely on your enthusiasm and vision. Sometimes, it can be difficult to know where to set your boundaries, or to accept that you have reached the limit of your abilities. When this card appears in a spread, it is quite likely that you have taken on too much and are finding it difficult to fulfil your commitments. If you are self-employed you might have so much work that you do not know how you will get it all done in time. If you are in paid employment, you may be working for someone who has very high expectations or who demands blood, sweat and tears from you. Perhaps it is difficult for you to say 'no' to people, because you are worried that this will reflect badly on you? You may be scared of setting personal limitations because these seem to cast doubt on your ability to cope. Yet by indiscriminately taking on everything that comes your way you will almost inevitably fail, which could damage your reputation even more.

Sometimes the burdens described by the Ten of Wands arrive as a direct result of your success. You have crossed one hurdle or attained a particular goal, and this immediately leads to the next set of challenges. For example, you might have pulled off a successful deal or business contract, so you now have to deliver your part of the bargain. This might involve a great deal more work and effort than you had imagined. If you have been promoted, you must now prove that you are worthy of your new position.

unable to see the wood for the trees

The illustration on this card shows a man carrying ten wands. He is holding them very awkwardly and they seem in danger of slipping out of his grasp at any minute. In addition, his face is pressed up against the wands so he cannot see what lies ahead. If only he held the wands in a different way, or even towed them in a cart, he would make life much easier for himself.

The Ten of Wands therefore asks whether you are making a rod for your own back in some way. Perhaps you have made the situation more complicated or difficult than necessary, yet you are unable to realise it. It may help to stand back from the situation in order to assess it objectively, so you know what you can achieve and what is too much for you. Once you see your position with more clarity, you might be able to plan a more effective coping strategy or ask someone to give you a hand. You are unlikely to get very far if you continue in your current vein.

PAGE of WANDS

page of wands

The Page of Wands shows that life is about to become busier for you. As with the other Pages, the Page of Wands can refer to either a person or to a situation.

as a situation

When it refers to a situation, the Page of Wands describes the beginning of an exciting new enterprise. It will stimulate your mind and you will enjoy watching things develop. It will be something that relates to the suit of Wands, so it might be a new business deal, an interesting negotiation, a change of direction in your career or some form of speculation. For example, you might decide to buy some property, especially if you intend to sell it on for a large profit rather than live in it yourself. Alternatively, you could become involved in an innovative scheme that you will have to sell to other people and which will test your initiative and intelligence. This might involve using your creativity, perhaps by writing a book and trying to sell it to a publisher. You will enjoy rising to the challenge. The surrounding cards will show how likely such ventures are to succeed.

The appearance of the Page of Wands in a spread indicates that your life is about to move at a faster pace. You may also have more contact with people than usual. For instance, you might make and receive more telephone calls than normal, or you could embark on plenty of short journeys such as weekend breaks or day trips. There will be a lot going on in your life, and you might extend or receive many invitations.

Wands are connected with travel, and very often the Page of Wands indicates that a holiday is on the horizon. If so, you may be visiting a hot country or a beach resort. This is especially likely if the card is accompanied by the Four of Swords, the Eight of Wands or the Knight of Wands. Sometimes, this card can indicate emigration to another country, but only if cards that symbolise radical change, such as the Wheel of Fortune, the World or Death, appear elsewhere in the spread.

as a person

When the Page of Wands refers to a person, they are faithful, loyal and trustworthy. They may be young, which is the traditional meaning of the Pages, or you might not know them very well at the time of the reading. They could also be a conscientious employee. They are enthusiastic, intuitive, creative and terrific company and may set your mind racing because they have so many interesting ideas.

Sometimes, this person is the bearer of exciting, challenging or unexpected news, in which case you might have to make plenty of last-minute preparations. For instance, a friend who lives overseas might get in touch and tell you that they will soon be visiting you. Alternatively, you could be sent on a business trip at short notice.

knight of wands

The Knight of Wands represents either a situation or a person. A great deal of excitement is involved, as is the promise of many interesting adventures. Travel is often indicated by this card, whether it is a holiday or emigration to another country. Life seems full of wonderful possibilities and opportunities.

as a situation

If this card describes a situation, it is one that is busy and bustling. You probably have high hopes that it will develop into something very exciting and stimulating, and which will lead you in new directions. Whether or not this happens will depend on the surrounding cards, since the Knight of Wands often promises more than it can deliver. Yet excited anticipation is an important part of new experiences, and you will certainly have plenty of that now.

This card has strong connections with travel, and its illustration shows a young man racing across a desert on a horse. There is a tremendous feeling of excitement and of covering vast distances. Therefore, the Knight of Wands can refer to a trip to another country, especially if the temperature will be hot or you will be in arid surroundings. Wands always carry a sense of adventure and exploration, so this card can suggest that you will be visiting somewhere for the first time.

The Knight of Wands can also refer to visitors from another country. They may come to stay with you, in which case your life will probably be completely wrapped up in theirs for the duration of their visit. This may be good fun at first but could become slightly wearing after a time, especially if they need a lot of entertaining.

Another form of travel suggested by the card involves moving house. If this is your plan, you may be considering moving far afield, especially if you are throwing caution to the winds in the process and settling in an area that you do not know very well. You are ready to take a gamble and see how it works out.

as a person

When describing a person, the Knight of Wands can refer to someone of either sex. They are probably quite young or have a very youthful quality. You may not know them very well, even if your relationship later develops. Alternatively, they might be in the process of leaving your life.

This person is great company because they are so lively, charming and entertaining. They are always brimming with interesting ideas and suggestions for new projects, even if these do not always see the light of day. In fact, they may be much better at hatching clever plans than seeing them through to a successful conclusion. They have an unpredictable streak so you cannot take them for granted. Some of their ideas may seem far-fetched at the time, although later on you can see the sense in them.

queen of wands

The Queen of Wands can represent a mature woman who is important to you at the time of the reading. Alternatively, the card may describe characteristics that you should adopt or develop within yourself.

the career woman

The Queen of Wands is an extremely capable woman who apparently has no difficulty in combining a successful career with a satisfying home life. She is able to juggle these two areas of her life with great aplomb, devoting a great deal of time and energy to each of them. Her home is likely to be decorated in a slightly quirky and eclectic style, and she may draw on influences from all over the world. This gives it warmth and individuality. The woman represented by the Queen of Wands is creative, too, whether in her personal or professional life. She probably dresses with flair and drama, and likes to be noticed. She is no shrinking violet. If you know her through your work, she is enthusiastic and good at making things happen.

She is interested in other people, which means she is deservedly popular. She is excellent company and has a wide circle of friends. She is sociable and gregarious, and a lively and intelligent conversationalist. It is easy for her to express her emotions, and she can be very passionate when the occasion demands it. She is loving and warm, but does not appreciate any form of possessiveness. In fact, she will nip it in the bud very quickly.

The Queen of Wands is an excellent hostess who enjoys creating an easy and harmonious atmosphere for friends and family. She is quite protective of loved ones and will stand up for them when she thinks it is necessary. She will also offer them encouragement when she considers they need it, and may be quite vociferous on the subject.

confidence and maturity

This woman is confident enough to follow her own path in life. She has an independent mind and is unlikely to slavishly follow fashions or trends. Instead, she has her own very definite tastes and enjoys expressing them. No matter what her age, she has maturity and sensitivity.

The Queen of Wands is capable of showing great compassion and understanding, but she does not suffer fools gladly. If she thinks someone has stepped out of line, or abused her trust, she will say so. Nevertheless, she may act as confidante to many people because of her combination of sympathy and common sense. If you tell her about your problems she will do her best to help you to find a solution.

No matter where this woman lives, she has a great love of the countryside and of nature. She may be particularly fond of cats. If she gardens, she will enjoy creating a garden full of drama, colour and geometrical shapes.

king of wands

The King of Wands describes a mature man who is important to you at the time of the reading. Alternatively, the card may describe certain personality traits that you should develop within yourself.

good humour

The man represented by the King of Wands has a terrific sense of humour. It may be one of the first things you notice about him and which attracts you to him. He is warm, lively, enthusiastic and vibrant, making you feel good when you are with him. As a result he is very popular and could be in great demand socially. He is friendly and talkative, and it is easy to get to know him.

One of his most marked characteristics is his infectious enthusiasm. He is always being swept up by fresh interests, into which he pours a great deal of energy. It may be quite difficult to keep up with him in these, because many of them do not last for long. Nevertheless, he does not let this hold him back and he may end up spending a lot of money on each pursuit before becoming tired of it and moving on to something else.

One area in which he never loses interest is his family. Despite his enormous charm, an occasional roving eye and possible sex appeal, this man is probably happily committed to a long-term partner. He enjoys family life, with all the emotional comforts that it entails. Even if he is not a father, he exudes a paternal energy which encourages people to confide in him and look up to him. Friends instinctively turn to him when they are in trouble because he is genuinely concerned about them.

If this man is a potential lover, be very careful because he may promise more than he can ever deliver. He probably means it all at the time, but he can then get cold feet and start to withdraw from the situation. He is particularly wary of anyone who is possessive or clingy. He enjoys creating intense friendships that teeter on the edge of sexual involvement, so they have fleeting episodes of tantalising intimacy that fan the flames of excitement. However, he may be reluctant to take things any further than this, especially if his heart lies elsewhere. The King of Wands is very seductive, but at his worst he can be a heartbreaker.

a successful businessman

The King of Wands has a successful career, especially if he acts as some form of adviser. He may take this in his stride and not let it affect him, or he might allow it to go to his head, so he comes across as self-important, over-confident and morally superior. His ability to see at least two sides to every argument makes him a skilled negotiator or arbitrator. He is likely to be respected for what he does, and is considered to be an authority figure. He may also be involved in a spiritual pursuit or practice.

pentacles

ACE of PENTACLES

ace of pentacles

All the Aces signify the start of something new, and the Ace
of Pentacles describes the beginning of a material venture
that will bring prosperity or a rise in status. It is a very
positive and exciting card because it heralds the arrival of so
many possibilities. Nevertheless, you will manage to keep
your feet on the ground because Pentacles is a very solid
and sensible suit.

 The traditional meaning of the Ace of Pentacles is an
engagement or marriage, since these were so often
accompanied by dowries. Indeed, they still are in some
cultures. Therefore, this card can refer to an emotional
alliance, especially if gifts such as rings are exchanged.
Sometimes, it can describe a relationship in which one or
both partners will profit financially, perhaps because material
wealth will be shared.

an enterprising start

This is an excellent card if you are considering going into business with someone or will be pooling your material resources with them in some way. It suggests that the venture will go well and the business will flourish, although you must look carefully to see if the surrounding cards tell a different story. For instance, if this card is accompanied by the Moon there may be some element of deceit or confusion involved.

This is a very encouraging card if you are thinking of buying a new home or of expanding or improving your current residence so it will be more comfortable. Pentacles rule solid plans and realities, so this Ace hints at success if you are spending money on property in which you will live. It does not refer to buying property for speculation, which is the province of Wands.

If you are thinking of changing jobs because you want something that increases your status or enhances your reputation, the Ace of Pentacles suggests that your plans will work out well. Alternatively, you might soon meet someone who will be influential or who has some important contacts, and who will be able to pull strings on your behalf. You may even deliberately cultivate them so they can help you in this way. This card can sometimes indicate the start of a practical commitment in which you will be involved, especially if this entails plenty of routine work or you have undertaken to do something week in, week out.

a windfall

Pentacles is the suit of money so there is a chance that you will receive a windfall or financial gift if this card appears in a spread. It may not be the answer to all your prayers but it will certainly improve your finances in some way. You might even receive a promotion at work that enhances your status while also increasing your income. If you enjoy rummaging around junk or antique shops, you might find an item that turns out to be worth more than you paid for it.

two of pentacles

This card shows that some form of balancing act is needed. You must juggle two elements of your life in order to keep things afloat. For example, you may have to balance the needs of your family against your work commitments, or you could be involved in a project that takes up so much of your leisure time that there is little to spare for anything else. Although it will be difficult to cope, you will manage to do so even if it involves a lot of energy.

sailing on choppy waters

The card shows a young man holding two coins which are linked together with a strip of fabric that bears a strong resemblance to the symbol for infinity. He holds one coin higher than the other, suggesting that one part of his life has ascendancy over the other. Behind him, two ships are sailing on very high seas. The message of the Two of

Pentacles is therefore very clear: you are busily trying to juggle life's ups and downs. Although it may be difficult to do this, you will succeed.

Sometimes this card describes a situation in which you are desperately trying to make ends meet. It seems that no sooner have you paid one set of bills than the next batch arrives. You may be paid on one day and have to spend most of that money on day-to-day living expenses the next. It is all a grind, and there is little chance to do anything more exciting, but it is simply a phase you are going through. This type of situation is especially likely if you have recently taken out a large loan in order to buy something and you now have to pay it back. For instance, you may be struggling with a large mortgage. You know that buying a property offers you a good investment but it is quite a burden at first.

The Two of Pentacles can also describe a situation in which your hands are full with practical commitments and you have very little time for other areas of your life. You might be looking after a small child who occupies most of your day, so everything else has to take second place. Your social life may have to go on the back-burner for the time being because you do not have the energy for it. Nevertheless, bringing up your child is very rewarding and you know that it will strengthen the bonds between the two of you.

hard work

The Two of Pentacles can also describe a situation in which your job takes up most of your time. Alternatively, you may have entered a profession in which the pay is very poor at first but will improve if you stick it out. You might be involved in some form of apprenticeship which you hope will lead to improved job prospects and an enhanced reputation.

If you are working with colleagues, the Two of Pentacles reveals the ups and downs that are almost inevitably involved. Your relationship with a workmate could be going through a difficult phase but this card suggests that you will manage to navigate your way through it.

three of pentacles

The Three of Pentacles is a card of encouragement. It is telling you that a venture has got off to a good start and it is now time to develop it. You have laid the foundations for something that can grow and, if you continue to take care of it, it will become a success.

developing a working partnership

Very often, this card describes being able to develop a solid, working partnership with someone. You have got over any initial teething troubles, such as understanding each other's foibles and getting to know one another better, and you are now ready to take things on to the next stage where you have a more instinctive and trusting relationship. This can also apply if you have recently had a disagreement with a colleague or client, and are wondering whether you can restore the peace. The Three of Pentacles suggests that you can, especially if you act professionally for the time being in order to make the situation less personal.

Sometimes, the Three of Pentacles describes being offered a more rewarding or lucrative job because of what you have achieved so far. You have proved yourself in some way and you are now in a position to reap the rewards of past efforts. This job may even arrive because someone has recommended you rather than because you applied for it. It is unlikely that you are about to reach the pinnacle of your career but you are certainly on the right path. If you are self-employed, this card can indicate that you will soon be offered an important contract that will increase your self-esteem or turn out to be an auspicious career move. Boosts like these to your career, income or reputation are especially likely if the Three of Pentacles is accompanied by the Six of Wands or Justice, both of which emphasise the theme of being rewarded for previous efforts.

establishing a secure home

If you are in the throes of creating a comfortable home, this card is encouraging you to carry on the good work, which could involve buying new furniture or making structural changes. It might be a good idea to employ a builder or architect to help you to improve the property, because you will benefit from their professional expertise. If you need to complete some official forms before work can begin, it is crucial that you do so.

It will also be important that you consult the other people who will be living in the property, to make sure that everyone agrees about what is being planned. Taking extra care at this stage will ensure that the project is successful and that you do not have to waste time later on sorting out things that should have been tackled now. However, it is useful to remember that Pentacles rule solid financial propositions rather than speculation, which is the area of Wands, so this card is not encouraging you to take risks with property in the hope that you will get your money back. Instead, it describes spending money on the property in which you live, so you can enjoy the benefits.

four of pentacles

This is a card with a dual message. It describes a sense of financial security, such as the reassurance that comes from knowing there is money in the bank. Yet it also warns against being so wrapped up in material affairs that you become reluctant to take risks or you want to keep your money to yourself. Such a lack of financial generosity may also indicate a lack of emotional generosity.

financial security

When the Four of Pentacles represents financial security, it is the sort that has been earned through hard work and responsibility. Your plans have worked out well or your career has become financially rewarding. You may not be making money hand over fist but nevertheless you are relatively comfortable and you have most of the things you need. You are in a stable position. Your reaction to this will be described by other cards that appear in the reading. For instance, if this card is accompanied by the Four of Cups, it suggests that you are feeling stale and slightly bored with your situation, and you are looking for excitement. On the other hand, if it appears with the Four of Wands you are probably feeling contented and happy.

hoarding your resources

There is, of course, another meaning to the Four of Pentacles. This describes a reluctance to risk your financial status and a desire to hold on to everything you own. This may be because you have recently struggled to make ends meet and are now worried about incurring the same problems again. Perhaps you are being careful with your money as opposed to downright mean. However, it is important to be aware of your attitude to your material possessions because you could fall into the trap of telling yourself that you cannot afford to spend money on any extras at all, even when this is not true. This is called 'poverty consciousness', and is a state of mind in which you focus on what you lack instead of what you have. Not only is this rather miserable, you can also convince yourself that you are worse off than you really are. If you persist in such thinking you may eventually discover that it is a self-fulfilling prophecy.

Occasionally, this reluctance to spend money can turn to avarice or miserliness. If this does not apply to you, you might meet such an attitude in someone else. This person could be obsessed with how much everything costs, even to the point of working out the value of the gifts they receive. This might be the sort of person who has always 'forgotten' to bring their money when it is their turn to buy a round of drinks, or who happily enjoys your hospitality but never returns it. It is more than likely that they are as stingy with their affections as they are with their money, making them an uncomfortable person to be around. If you are considering going into some form of partnership with them, you could well find that you do all the giving while they do all the taking.

five of pentacles

In the tarot, all the fives are difficult cards. The Five of
Pentacles warns against being so wrapped up in one area
of your life that you ignore the others and suffer some form
of loss as a result. This might mean losing someone's
affection because it has to take second place to other
concerns, or becoming so focused on materialism that you
do not have time to enjoy life's more simple pleasures.

impoverishment

This card carries the illustration of a young couple trudging
through the snow. The woman's feet are bare. She is
bundled up against the weather but her thin clothes offer
scant protection. The man beside her hobbles along on
crutches. Above them is a stained glass window, vibrant
with colour, but they have not noticed it. The couple appear
to have been neglected by society and are struggling to

survive. This image underlines the Five of Pentacles'
message of potential loss and impoverishment.

Sometimes this card appears in a spread when you are
feeling one step removed from everyone around you. This
might be because everyone else seems to be better off,
more confident or have fewer worries than you or you may
be missing out on your social life because your work keeps
you so busy or because you simply cannot afford many
outside interests at the moment. It could feel as though life
has lost much of its richness and variety, and your focus has
narrowed down to drudgery, financial worries and a sense of
isolation. If you are facing an onerous task, it may feel like a
mountain that you will never be able to climb.

You might also feel rather sorry for yourself. When this
happens, it can be tempting to start seeing yourself as a
martyr or as someone who deserves everyone's sympathy
and special treatment. As a result, you may refuse offers of
help because it somehow seems more noble to struggle on
by yourself. Alternatively, you could be feeling so alone that
it seems improbable that anyone would want to help you
and so you do not even ask. If you are struggling to make
ends meet when you draw this card, it is questioning
whether you have explored every avenue open to you. You
might be entitled to allowances or benefits, but you will not
know about these until you make enquiries.

remedying the situation

Five is a number of change in the tarot, so the difficult situation
you are undergoing will not last for ever. It may even be a
catalyst for positive change, perhaps when you realise that
you do not have to put up with these conditions or
circumstances any longer and you are going to do something
constructive about them. It may be that all you need is to take
more care of yourself, to treat yourself better or to allow
yourself some time off from the daily grind. You might realise
that you are putting a relationship in jeopardy because you are
not paying enough attention to it, and can therefore manage
to save it before you lose something infinitely precious.

six of pentacles

The Six of Pentacles describes giving or receiving money. You might finally receive money that is owed to you, or you could be the recipient of someone's unexpected largesse. Alternatively, you might be the donor.

Although Pentacles is a suit that rules money and material possessions, your emotions have an important bearing on the interpretation of this card. How do you feel about receiving or giving this money? Are you grateful, resentful or do you feel obligated in some way?

kindness or condescension

If you are on the receiving end of some money, how does this feel? You may be pleased because you are in need of financial help or because you are being paid for services rendered. You might simply take the money and think nothing more about it. If someone is being kind or is giving you something that they know you want, you might be touched by their consideration and want to thank them. You might even want to reciprocate the gesture in future if possible.

However, there is a possibility with this card that you may feel slightly patronised. The person giving you the money may make it clear that they are in a position of power and you should be grateful for any crumbs that fall from their table in your direction. This may apply even if you have earned the money they are giving you, or if they are repaying a debt. Somehow, they might manipulate the situation into one of power and subservience.

It is important to remember this if you are the one who is handing out the money or possessions. Are you being condescending or haughty? Are you giving the impression that the recipient should somehow be beholden to you?

Alternatively, you may feel duty-bound to give someone some money or belongings, even if you do not really want to. This situation could arise if you have to take care of a relative or friend who has fallen on hard times and needs your help. You might feel an obligation to give them what they need, even though this stirs up feelings of resentment or you think the money could be better spent on yourself. You could even suspect that this person has come to view you as a soft touch and that they would be quite able to manage without your help if they wanted to.

not getting enough

Sometimes, the Six of Pentacles describes the feeling that you are not getting your fair share of something. You might be envious of someone else's financial status and wish that you could be so lucky. If you have been waiting for a debt to be repaid, a grant to be allocated or a credit to be honoured, you could be annoyed to discover that you have not received everything that is owed to you or that you think you deserve. This raises the question of whether your expectations were too high or you are justified in feeling hard-done-by. The surrounding cards will help to clarify this.

seven of pentacles

When this card appears in a spread it is telling you that you have made a lot of progress but you still have a long way to go. Nevertheless, you are justified in feeling pleased with yourself and you may even want to rest on your laurels for a short while before starting work again. Perhaps you deserve a holiday, or you might even be considering taking a sabbatical.

The Seven of Pentacles is also reminding you not to take your skills and abilities for granted, nor to denigrate them through false modesty. Instead, think of fresh ways to use them, even if these take you in new and uncharted directions. This might also be a time when you can profit from all your hard work and begin to reap the rewards of everything you have accomplished so far.

starting afresh

In the tarot, the number seven can signify the end of a cycle, and so the Seven of Pentacles can describe reaching the end of one stage in your life and beginning another. You might consider embarking on a new business venture which will be something of a departure for you or which will encourage you to display talents that have not been put to the test before. For example, you might be thinking about leaving paid employment and becoming self-employed. The reputation and experience that you have already accumulated will help you to win new clients, but being self-employed will mean you have to develop the skills needed to run a business.

Alternatively, you may be thinking about selling your current home and buying somewhere else, especially if this new house will be smaller or cheaper so you can reduce your outgoings. Although it may be a wrench to leave your present home, you can look forward to the challenge of creating a new one.

developing new talents

This card is encouraging you to assess all your talents and abilities, even if they are not related to business or money. Weigh up your mental skills and your emotional strengths. These could be very useful if you were thinking about doing some charity work or helping in a voluntary organisation and you will also be able to draw on them if you are contemplating starting a family. If this card appears when you are considering returning to work after a spell of unemployment, perhaps during which you were bringing up your children, you should think carefully about everything you have to offer a prospective employer. You may feel daunted by what seems to be a tremendous challenge but the Seven of Pentacles is encouraging you to do your best.

Although Pentacles governs money, it also rules ventures that have emotional, mental or spiritual value for you. It can therefore describe becoming engrossed in a pastime that will give you a great deal of satisfaction. This may not earn you any money, nor may you want it to, although the Seven of Pentacles does not rule out that possibility for the future.

eight of pentacles

We all have different skills, abilities and talents, and the Eight of Pentacles is encouraging you to explore them and trust in them. It is a very strong reminder that everyone has something to offer, even if it seems unusual or is not valued by society as a whole. You might be interested in a subject that is generally ridiculed or considered unimportant, but the Eight of Pentacles is telling you to ignore such constraints. Instead, you should work on whatever helps to satisfy you and make you the person you are.

the courage to be yourself

The Eight of Pentacles asks us to be ourselves, no matter who or what that might be. The illustration shows a young man hammering out a design on a circular object. It is a five-pointed star on a coin, which is the symbol of Pentacles. If you look closely, you will see that each pentacle is slightly different. Only one is completely symmetrical: all the rest might be considered imperfect by comparison, yet they are charming in their own way. Who is to say that one of them is better than another?

This is a strong reminder not to feel diminished by what makes you unique to the people around you. There might be some obvious physical differences that make you feel self-conscious, and by which some people may try to judge you. Alternatively, it could be something more subtle, such as an unconventional way of looking at the world, a quirky sense of humour or a belief system that no one else shares. This is part of what makes you who you are, and the Eight of Pentacles is telling you to have the confidence to express it.

an apprenticeship

Sometimes the Eight of Pentacles describes the ability to learn something new. This might be a leisure pursuit or craft that will bring you a great deal of enjoyment in your spare time. On the other hand, it could be a training or apprenticeship in a skill that you hope eventually to develop into a full-time career. If you are considering embarking on such a path at the time of the reading, this card is encouraging you to do so and suggests that it will be a very fruitful enterprise.

Pentacles are associated with money, so there is a chance that you will make money at this. Yet whether or not that happens, you will also gain the satisfaction of learning something new and developing skills and techniques as a result. You might also enhance your reputation, even if it is only as someone who has the courage to try something new.

The suggestion that you should learn new talents and abilities is especially pertinent if you left school long ago and have been making your way in the world for some time. You are now at a stage where you will enjoy expanding your horizons in whichever way appeals most. This is emphasised if the card is accompanied by the Seven of Pentacles, the Ace of Swords or Pentacles, or the Sun.

nine of pentacles

This is a card of satisfaction, achievement and happiness, especially where your material needs are concerned. It indicates that you have reached a point in your life where everything is going well and you have most of the things you require. It can appear in a spread when you have succeeded materially and have a great deal to show for all your past efforts. If you have been going through a difficult time it can suggest that your situation will soon improve, possibly in quite dramatic ways.

justified pride

The Nine of Pentacles often appears in a reading when you have good reason to feel proud of everything you have accomplished. For instance, you may have worked very hard all your life to attain a comfortable lifestyle, an attractive home or many status symbols. They are all outward manifestations of your inner achievements and strength of mind, and you are justified in feeling proud of them. The card may appear at a time when you are considering spending money on some expensive objects, such as a new car, luxurious clothes, costly furniture or jewellery. These will all say something about your place in the world and your ability to provide for yourself and your family. It is highly likely that none of this has come cheap and that you have worked hard for everything you now have. You have not achieved prosperity through sheer accident.

moving house

This is one of the cards that can refer to a house move, especially if you will be moving to a property that is in beautiful surroundings or which has a large garden. It is likely to be a very beneficial move and you will gain from it in many ways. The Nine of Pentacles can also encourage you to increase your contact with nature, especially if you will be working with it in some way. For example, you might enjoy growing your own fruit or vegetables, or cultivating grapes with which to make your own wine if you live in a suitable part of the world.

receiving a windfall

Sometimes this card describes being in the happy position of benefiting from an unexpected windfall. Alternatively, it can indicate that you will receive some other form of bonus or perk. If you are thinking about selling one home and buying another, you might make a substantial profit on the deal.

standing on your own two feet

The Nine of Pentacles can also appear in a spread when you have reached the point where you can support yourself and you do not have to rely on other people for financial help. You are now able to make your own way in the world. You may even be able to assist other people who are just starting out in life, perhaps by providing them with a home.

ten of pentacles

This card has a very simple meaning because it indicates material satisfaction and a happy family life. Ten is the number of culmination in the tarot, so the card describes the attainment of something that you have been striving for. However, it asks the question 'What next?' You have reached the end of one cycle and are now ready to move on to the next. But what will it be?

family happiness

If this card appears in a reading when life has been difficult and you have been struggling to tolerate your partner, or even to stay together as a family, it is reassuring you that the situation will soon improve markedly. This is especially likely if it is accompanied by the Star, Temperance, the Sun or the Ten of Cups. Worries will melt away as you find the courage to face up to them and the problems between you will be resolved.

If you have been thinking about moving in with a lover or marrying them, once again this card offers encouragement. You will enjoy the process of creating a home with them, and of everything that this entails.

ancestral lines

When the Ten of Pentacles describes material comfort and a secure financial base, these have often been passed down through the generations. For instance, you may come into an inheritance or you might live in what has always been the family home. You may be given a valuable heirloom or be asked to take care of something that will be kept in the family for years to come. This card therefore differs from the Nine of Pentacles, which describes the material satisfaction that comes from your own efforts, because the Ten of Pentacles can refer to receiving money through other people, purely because of your association with them.

This card does not always refer to a financial inheritance. It might describe a skill that has been handed down from one generation to the next, and from which you can earn money. If you are going through a difficult time, the Ten of Pentacles suggests asking your family for financial support or practical help. This is a good opportunity to rely on your relatives and to trust that they will do what they can for you.

a house move

Sometimes this card indicates a house move. If so, you are probably moving to an older property or one that has plenty of history attached to it. It might also be a property that was originally used for business purposes. The Ten of Pentacles is one of the most positive cards in the entire deck, so this is likely to be a favourable move unless the surrounding cards say otherwise. It may also turn out to be a very good investment.

page of pentacles

The Page of Pentacles can refer either to a situation or to a person. Material matters, physical reality or practicalities are involved and may need plenty of care and attention until they are more established.

as a situation

If the Page of Pentacles refers to a situation, it is one that has only recently begun. It is in its early stages and therefore needs to be carefully nurtured if it is to develop in the way you wish. For example, this might be the start of an important phase in your life, when you hope to build successfully on the foundations that you lay down now. You are at the planning stage, and your actions can make all the difference between success and failure.

Very often, the Page of Pentacles indicates that you will soon hear some interesting news which will affect your material status in some way. You might discover that some money is on its way to you, although you do not have it yet. This is unlikely to be a large sum unless other financial cards, such as the Ace of Pentacles, also appear in the reading. Alternatively, you could hear of a job that sounds suitable for you, so you must now think about applying for it and presenting yourself in the best possible light. If you are hoping to move house but have not yet found the perfect place, you might soon be given information about somewhere that sounds ideal and you will have to consider how best to pursue this. You could also be given some useful information about a potential investment, especially if you will be getting involved in its early stages.

If life has been rather difficult recently, you may hear some good news that sets your mind at rest. For instance, if you have been anxiously looking for a job, you could be given something that will tide you over until something better comes along. If you have recently taken an exam or test, you might be delighted with the results.

as a person

When the Page of Pentacles describes a person, it is a young man or woman. Nevertheless, they may appear to be much more mature than their real age would suggest, and they could have a responsible job that is connected with finance or property. They may also be very grounded in reality, making them matter-of-fact and sensible. You feel you can trust them, particularly if they are a business associate or will be selling you something. They may be either entering or leaving your life.

This person is diligent, capable, efficient and practical. They could be a successful administrator because they are so good at tackling routine duties and keeping track of facts. However, they do not have much imagination and you may not want to spend too much time in their company. Perhaps that would be inappropriate, given the nature of your relationship with them; they might be a colleague who you only meet every now and then, or they could be your estate agent or solicitor. Nevertheless, there is a solidity and dependability to them that you value and can trust.

knight of pentacles

The Knight of Pentacles has two main meanings. It can
represent either a situation or a person and in both cases, it
is connected with material matters, practicalities and
established ideas.

as a situation

The other Knights of the Minor Arcana describe situations
that happen quickly, but the Knight of Pentacles is very
different. The illustration on the card shows a young man
dressed in heavy armour, which in itself must restrict his
movements. Instead of galloping along in the style of the
other horses on the Knight cards, this horse is standing
stock-still, all four feet planted on the ground. Its black colour
underlines the feeling of solidity that accompanies this card.

Therefore, the Knight of Pentacles indicates a situation
that has come to a temporary halt. You may have reached

an impasse with someone, so all you can do is bide your time and wait for things to start moving again. Perhaps you are determined to stand your ground and not give way on matters that challenge your principles or moral ethics. Alternatively, if this card describes your day-to-day work, perhaps you are feeling stuck in a rut and thoroughly bored. The pay may be good but the creative satisfaction may be minimal. You might be coping with the dead hand of bureaucracy when this card appears, so your options are restricted or you cannot make any further progress without an official stamp of approval.

This card can also suggest a less stagnant situation in which you are simply working away at whatever needs to be done. You may be very busy with the practicalities of daily life, such as paying the bills, keeping the money coming in and simply getting on with the necessities. It can also show the ability to gradually work towards the achievement of a goal or ambition, especially when coping with the hard slog and the sheer perseverance that this entails.

as a person

When the Knight of Pentacles describes a person, they are relatively young and they may not be especially important to you. They are practical, determined, capable and painstaking, and you feel you can trust them. However, they might also give the impression of being rather stolid and dull. They could be rather complacent, unimaginative or prosaic, too, so they are not always very exciting company. They may also be wedded to tradition, and afraid of bucking trends or departing from convention. They prefer to do things by the book rather than take risks or think for themselves. Nevertheless, you know where you stand with them, and you may have good reason to feel grateful for their solidity. If they are a lover, they are faithful, honest and steadfast. Once they get to know you and feel they can trust you, you may be surprised by their depth of passion and sensuality.

queen of pentacles

The Queen of Pentacles describes a mature woman who is important to you at the time of the reading. Alternatively, the card is encouraging you to express some of the personality traits that belong to the Queen of Pentacles.

the hard worker

The woman described by the Queen of Pentacles is not afraid of hard work. She throws herself into it wholeheartedly, for she has faith in her own abilities and knows that she does a good job. She is a staunch believer that we all have to help ourselves in life, and that there is no such thing as a free lunch. She is a steadfast worker who will work round the clock if necessary in order to complete a job on time. Nevertheless, there is no danger of her being exploited or taken for a ride, and she is perfectly able to stand up for herself when necessary. She is quite capable of ticking off colleagues if she thinks they are not pulling their weight or are jeopardising a project. She also knows how to enjoy herself when her work is finished, and she has the money to be able to do so.

Sometimes, this woman may be involved in the family business, so there might be a sense that her job was pre-ordained for her and she did not have much say in the matter. Tradition and family values are very important to her, so she is reluctant to alter what she believes to be the natural order of things. Her work involves financial matters and investments, property and the land, or anything else connected with physical reality.

Money is very important to this woman and she spends it wisely. She is very shrewd and clever when making investments, and considers it important to put her money to good use. If she has it, she likes to spend it on items that will grow in value over the years or which will provide a sense of comfort and security for her family. If she can afford to buy the best, she will. She can see no point in stinting herself by buying inferior goods, and also believes that these reflect badly on her. Her appreciation of the good things in life means that her home is extremely comfortable and might even be lavish. There is a sense of opulence and abundance; she is attracted to natural fabrics and rich colours.

If this woman has money to spare, she is very generous with it. However, she does not part with it in order for it to be wasted, so she may place conditions on her financial gifts. She is charitable and altruistic. She gives practical help when someone is in trouble, rather than purely emotional support.

family values

Home and family are essential to this woman's happiness, and she will do her utmost to create a stable family life. When looking for a partner, she is drawn to people who are reliable, dependable and faithful. She needs someone who complements her sensuality and passion, and who she can trust.

KING of PENTACLES

king of pentacles

The King of Pentacles describes a mature man who is important to you at the time of the reading. Alternatively, the card denotes certain personality traits that you should develop within yourself.

a successful man

The illustration on the card shows a man holding a golden orb in one hand and a large pentacle in the other. In addition to these obvious signs of monetary success, he wears a highly decorated crown and is sitting on an ornate throne. A large castle in the background is further testament to his financial and material status. The King of Pentacles is therefore a man with solid prosperity behind him. He is probably involved in some form of business, especially if it is connected with property, finance, real estate or the building trade. He works hard and the material results speak for themselves. He may even have the Midas touch when it comes to business deals or investments, so he apparently cannot help making money.

Once he has attained some measure of wealth, the King of Pentacles knows how to keep it. He is a canny investor with an eye for a sound deal and a good rate of return. Nevertheless, he is quite cautious financially and will not do anything to risk his own security and that of his family. He has worked too hard to get where he is to run the risk of throwing it all away on get-rich-quick schemes.

The King of Pentacles is doubtless in charge of other people, and is a good leader. He sets an excellent example, even if he lacks the creativity and verve to capture other people's imaginations. Instead, he teaches them to take things slowly and to make steady progress over time. He may even work for years, in determined fashion, before he reaches the position he has always imagined for himself. He does not mind this because it reassures him that he has attained his position through decent hard work, so he can feel proud of what he has achieved.

a loyal friend

There is something very solid, dependable and reliable about the King of Pentacles. He is someone you can trust, and he has great strength of character. What he lacks in vision and innovative flair he makes up for in fidelity, tenderness and devotion. He is a sensual lover, although he is reluctant to take emotional risks and so will not declare his feelings until he is absolutely certain that his affections will not be rejected. However, he can be rather jealous or possessive when he feels threatened.

When the King of Pentacles describes character traits that should be developed, these are the ability to be content with your lot, and to be thankful for the blessings that have been bestowed on you. You are also being encouraged to draw on the emotional strength that your family and friends provide.

cups

ace of cups

This is a glorious card, one of the most positive in the entire tarot. As with all the Aces, it signifies new beginnings and the chance to start afresh and, as it belongs to the suit of Cups, it describes the start of an emotional relationship, a fulfilling activity, a spiritual pursuit or anything else that will have meaning for you. Sometimes it can signify a birth, such as the birth of a child or a creative project. It may indicate the beginning of a very happy and enjoyable phase in your life, which you will look back on with great affection.

a sense of optimism

If life has been difficult when this card appears in a spread, it is reassuring you that the situation will soon improve. This may not happen magically of its own accord and you might have to help matters along in some way, but you can look forward to a more peaceful or happy time in the future. If there has been a rift in a relationship, the card is encouraging you to make amends, even if that means being the first one to say sorry. There is so much to be gained from doing this that it would be churlish to cling to your pride and wait for the other person to apologise first.

If you have recently met someone new and are wondering whether anything will come of your relationship, the Ace of Cups is a good indication that it will. It may develop into a fulfilling friendship that will last for many years or you might fall in love with each other. Even if the relationship does not last, it will be highly significant for you in some way. Sometimes this card can also describe an engagement or wedding, which will bring great happiness and emotional satisfaction.

birth

The Ace of Cups has associations with fertility, so it may indicate the birth of a child. This is especially likely if it is accompanied by the Empress, which is another card of fecundity. Alternatively, it can describe the beginning of a creative venture that will bring you much personal gratification and a strong sense of achievement. This may not necessarily be something that is recognised by everyone else as a great success, since such things are entirely personal and subjective. One person's triumph is another one's mediocre achievement.

abundance

The illustration on this card shows a cup running over, which describes the sense of abundance that accompanies the Ace of Cups. You might feel immense gratitude about something that happens to you, perhaps believing that you have been blessed or have received a special gift from a higher spiritual power. You could become involved in a project or venture that will offer you some wonderful opportunities, or the chance to grow more fully as a human being and to pass on some of what you have learned to other people.

two of cups

This is a card of partnership, communion and co-operation.
It signifies some form of togetherness and understanding,
whether this is present in a new relationship or is being
forged in an existing partnership. The Two of Cups is a
traditional indication of a contract or agreement and its
literal interpretation is of two hearts beating as one, or two
souls united in a common purpose.

forging a bond

This is a very positive and encouraging card when a
relationship is going through a difficult stage because it
describes the ability to put your differences behind you and
to concentrate instead on what brings you together. Some
measure of forgiveness may be needed here, of course, but
the Two of Cups suggests that you will manage to achieve
this. Other cards that appear in the same spread, such as

Judgement or Temperance, may underline this message and encourage you to put the past behind you.

The Two of Cups is a classic indication that a contract will soon be signed. Although Cups generally refer to emotional and spiritual matters, as well as anything else that carries a lot of meaning for the questioner, in this case the nature of the contract can be quite wide-ranging. For instance, it might be connected with a new home, a business alliance, a marriage or a financial arrangement. What is important is the level of emotion behind it, and the sense that everyone is working together to create a harmonious union.

In itself, however, the Two of Cups does not guarantee that everything will be hunky-dory. Harmony and unity will not magically materialise without any effort on your part, or that of the other people involved. In the Minor Arcana, any card numbered two indicates the beginning of something but it does not ensure that it will have a successful outcome. Instead, the Two of Cups is saying that you have made a promising start and have good reason to be optimistic. However, you should not be complacent, nor should you automatically expect someone else to do all the hard work while you take a back seat, unless you have specifically agreed that this will happen.

a satisfying relationship

If this card appears when you are wondering whether a budding relationship will develop in the way you wish, perhaps by becoming a satisfying love affair or even a committed partnership, it is assuring you that things will get off to a good start. Even so, do not expect the relationship to be completely untroubled because that is unlikely to happen. You may also have to guard against being overly idealistic about this person, perhaps painting them in a rosy light that is unrealistic or which has nothing to do with their true character.

The Cups suit has links with fertility, so the Two of Cups can sometimes refer to the birth of a child. If so, the relationship between child and parent will be strong and fulfilling. Occasionally, this card may indicate the birth of twins.

three of cups

There is often a reason to celebrate when this card appears.
You may be emerging from a trying phase, so you feel as
though you are coming out of the darkness into the
sunshine once more. You may have succeeded at a tricky
task or pulled off a difficult negotiation, so you have good
reason to feel pleased with yourself. Or you may simply be
celebrating some of the basic joys of life such as friendship
and companionship.

an excuse for a party

The illustration on this card shows women holding up
goblets, and one can almost hear the clink of glasses as
they meet in a toast. Indeed, the Three of Cups often refers
to some form of party. This could be a housewarming, a
celebration of the birth of a baby, an engagement party, a
wedding reception or an event to launch what will be a

successful creative enterprise. However, the card does not always refer to an elaborate or official celebration, so it might simply indicate sharing a bottle of champagne with one other person to toast some good news.

the comfort of friends

This card has strong associations with the joys of friendship, so it can sometimes describe the affection and contented familiarity that exists between people who have known each other for a long time. If life has been hard for you and you have felt as though you are struggling along single-handedly, the Three of Cups may be reminding you to turn to your close friends because they will be able to offer you the comfort and support that you need. Nevertheless, you might have to be selective about who you talk to, perhaps deliberately choosing someone who you know is a good listener.

If you have not seen or heard from a particular friend for some time, this card may well be encouraging you to make contact with them again, especially if they have been on your mind recently. Ignore any sense of awkwardness about being the one to make the first move and instead have the generosity of spirit that enables you to get in touch and see how they are. To your surprise, you may be able to renew your bonds of friendship with them and enjoy being in their company again.

solace

Sometimes the Three of Cups is a harbinger of good news. You could soon hear something that will make you sigh with relief or want to offer up a heartfelt prayer of thanks. A knotty problem may finally be resolved to your satisfaction, making you feel that once again life has a lot to offer and that it is not all doom and gloom. If you have been ill, for instance, you may now be well on the way to recovery. Perhaps you have been waiting for the outcome of some medical tests, and you might now hear the results you were hoping for rather than the ones you were dreading? This is especially likely if the Star or Strength also appear in the spread.

four of cups

There is a sense of stagnation, discontent and boredom when this card appears. You may be going through a phase in which nothing meets your expectations or life feels flat. You might struggle to work up the enthusiasm to do much at all, and achieve very little in the process. Perhaps you keep starting projects and then leaving them unfinished because you lack the energy to see them through to a conclusion. There may be a good reason for this, possibly because you are depressed and need help, or because you are exhausted after a long period of exertion or stress and you will not feel better until you have recuperated. This is especially likely if the Four of Cups is accompanied by the Four of Swords.

weary of the world

Very often, this card describes a sense of being jaded and stale. You may have recently experienced a very busy period in which a lot was happening, and now that things have calmed down again you are suffering from severe anti-climax. Life might seem colourless and dreary, with nothing more to offer you. When you feel like this you may wish to seek outside help if the condition persists for a long time or it begins to interfere with your life.

Sometimes the card refers to the feelings of lassitude and boredom, which can result when life has ceased to offer you any challenges. To outward appearances, you may appear to have everything that anyone could possibly want, such as a happy relationship, a lavish home, an overflowing bank account or a fantastic job. Yet it fails to give you any sort of mental or emotional satisfaction, so you feel uninterested, listless or stuck in a rut.

The Four of Cups can also describe the tedium that accompanies an uneventful phase in your life when nothing exciting seems to happen. It feels as though you plod from one day to the next, with little or no light relief. Yet does it have to be like this? Perhaps you need to exert yourself a little more, or maybe you must accept that this is just a phase and it will not last for ever.

There is also a chance that the Four of Cups refers to the disillusionment that can follow when someone has let you down or betrayed you in some way. You may have lost all faith in people because your trust has been abused, and you are bitterly telling yourself that you will never put yourself in this position again.

an opportunity beckons

Although this is a difficult period for you, it is important that you try to rise above it. If you do not, you may miss a worthwhile or exciting opportunity that comes your way. You must recognise this when it arrives, so it is essential that you remain aware of what is happening around you. Do not become so disillusioned or fed up that you cannot see what is under your nose, because it could be something fulfilling, stimulating or the very thing that will make you fall in love with life again.

five of cups

Some form of loss is associated with this card and it has filled you with regret or grief. However, you have not lost as much as you imagine, even though it may be difficult to accept this at the time. You are going through a dispiriting and possibly even bleak phase in which you cannot help but concentrate on what you have lost. Yet it is important to remember what you have retained from the situation; you may find that something can be salvaged from it, or that it contains benefits of which you are not yet aware.

Although this is a difficult card, it offers hope. The illustration shows a figure gazing at three overturned cups, while two stand upright behind them. The central message of this card is therefore that although something has been lost, something else has been saved or retained. Therefore, the situation is perhaps not as dire as it seems.

mourning

Sometimes the Five of Cups describes the period of mourning
that follows a bereavement. You may feel inconsolable and be
unable to think of anything except your loss. However, this card is
urging you to consider what you might have gained from the
situation or what has not been destroyed. For instance, if
someone has died, you still have your memories of them, even if
these are currently painful for you, and you can still remember the
warmth of the affection or love that existed between you. There
may also be a gift from this person, perhaps in the form of an
inheritance and, although this may never console you for your
loss, in time, there will be a need to accept that life must go on
and that even the most bitter grief can become easier to live with.

If you are trying to come to terms with a broken
relationship, the Five of Cups is suggesting that you will feel
better when you reflect on what you have gained as a result,
or what you have retained from the situation. For instance, you
may have managed to remain civil with each other and be
doing your utmost to act in everyone's best interests. You can
take pride in this. If it was an extremely difficult or
argumentative relationship, part of you may feel relieved to
have brought an end to so much tension and anger. You
might also have learned some valuable lessons about yourself
as a result of what has happened.

a flawed relationship

There are times when the Five of Cups refers to a partnership
that is not as fulfilling as you would wish. You may be separated
from one another, whether by physical distance or emotional
differences, which makes you sad or fills you with regret.
Perhaps you have been betrayed, making you feel that you can
never trust this person again. Or you may suspect that you have
grown apart and you have little in common any more. Should
you stay together or separate? Is your friendship with someone
continuing purely out of habit, because you are not sure if you
still like them? Yet in each of these cases, and in similar
circumstances, there might still be a link between you, which
you can develop and foster, given time.

six of cups

This card describes the power of the past. It may indicate a period in which you are caught up in memories and fond recollections of days gone by. It can also describe a tendency to live in the past rather than the present, especially if this means feeling very nostalgic about the way things used to be. There may be an eagerness to recreate history in the present, or a yearning to emulate a vanished way of life. You might encounter someone from your past, or you may get the chance to revive an old skill or technique and then profit from it.

the good old days

Very often, the Six of Cups describes a tendency to wear rose-coloured spectacles when thinking about the past. You could be unconsciously screening out any unpleasant memories and only concentrating on the happy ones. For instance, when thinking about your childhood it may seem that the summers were always gloriously hot and the winters always wonderfully snowy, although this was not always the case. Parents and other older relatives may be remembered as beacons of wisdom and kindness, rather than as human beings who were not as perfect as you like to think. Are you clinging to the past because the present is frightening or unwelcoming?

This card can also indicate a tendency to rewrite history, so that unpleasant incidents lose their sting or a difficult situation is given a happy ending. You may tell yourself that things were so much better in your day: the music was more melodious; the food was fresher; violence was almost unknown; comedy programmes were funnier; politicians could be respected. If this card is accompanied by the Moon, it may be a sign of some form of false memory syndrome or an entirely misplaced nostalgia. This can cause confusion at best, trouble at worst.

reviving old skills

The other meaning of the Six of Cups is that someone or something from your past will once again become important for you, and you will gain from the experience in some way. For instance, you might hear from a cherished friend or an old love. It will be enjoyable to catch up with each other and find out what has been happening since you last met. By itself, this card does not say whether this partnership will be revived or whether you will lose touch with each other again. However, if it appears with any of the cards that describe love, such as the Ace of Cups, the Sun or the Star, you might be right in assuming that you will pick up the threads of your old relationship again.

Sometimes, the Six of Cups is encouraging you to brush up on old talents and to use them again. This could involve rediscovering a previous hobby that you have neglected recently, or it might mean reviving a particular skill that you have not used for a long time and putting it to good use once more. This card can also describe finding something old, such as an antique, that turns out to be valuable. For instance, if you are sorting through cupboards or browsing in a junk shop, you might stumble across something that is worth some money or which will bring you a great deal of pleasure.

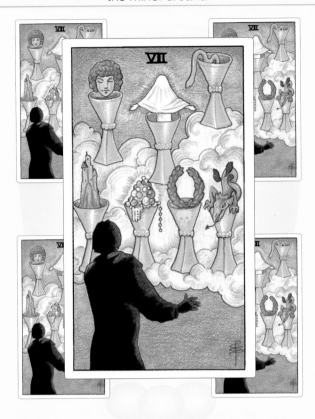

seven of cups

This card is full of promise and openings. It is telling you that you will soon be spoilt for choice in some way. You will be offered several opportunities, which could all seem exciting or encouraging. However, some of these will fail to live up to expectations and a few might even turn out to be liabilities or more trouble than they are worth. Nevertheless, at least one opportunity will be extremely favourable, and it might even lead on to tremendous success, happiness or contentment.

You will also have to exert a great deal of effort in order to get the most out of these opportunities, so you cannot expect anything beneficial simply to land in your lap without any hard work on your part. Nevertheless, if you are prepared to do your best, you will look back on this time as a period in which you were able to realise a dream or achieve something very worthwhile.

making a careful choice

The card shows seven cups floating in the air while a shadowy figure stands in front of them and is apparently in the act of choosing some of them. At first glance, each cup may look attractive and shiny, ripe for the picking. However, when you look more closely you realise that some of the cups contain rather unpleasant objects, or the reflections on their curved surfaces are strangely reminiscent of skulls or bombs. The card is therefore warning you to look very carefully at the options that are on offer to you, and not to reach automatically for whatever seems most auspicious, remunerative or golden. Something that appears to be the brightest or biggest may not necessarily be what is best for you.

You may encounter this situation in a relationship. For instance, you might find that you are in great demand and that several would-be partners are interested in you at the same time. Which one should you choose, if indeed you should choose any of them? One may have a lot of money, which you find attractive, but could turn out to have a filthy temper. Another might be uninterested in worldly concerns, which you think is endearing, but later on you might discover that they have no interest in fidelity, either. In the end, you may become involved with someone who perhaps did not seem very appealing at first or whom you almost discounted, but who makes you happy.

wishful thinking

The Seven of Cups warns against wishful thinking, indulging in whims or concentrating on daydreams that will never amount to anything. Although the card describes the promise of something, it insists that you should be very hard-headed when making a decision about it. You must not choose something with scant regard for how it will turn out, nor should you assume that it will work out well of its own accord. You may have to deal with problems associated with your choices, or put in a huge amount of effort before you see any rewards. However, if things do work out, you will be delighted with what has been achieved.

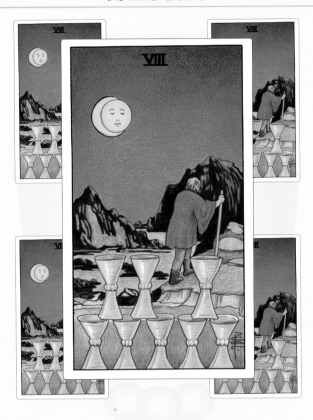

eight of cups

The main themes of this card are abandonment and endings. Something has reached the end of its natural cycle and it is time to move away from it. Very often this involves a turning point in a relationship, when you realise that it has run its course and nothing more can be gained from it. Although this can be very difficult or even heart-rending at the time, the Eight of Cups carries a sense of inevitability. There is a feeling that you have no other options. There is also the promise, even if it remains unspoken, that happier times will follow.

the end of a cycle

The finality associated with this card can seem uncompromising and bleak. It often describes a relationship or situation that is a spent force. For instance, it may be a bloodless marriage in which both partners no longer have anything in common, so one of the partners finally plucks up the courage to end it and begin again. Outsiders may wonder why, since on the surface the couple got on so well together or appeared to share such a contented life. This might well happen when the couple's children leave home and they become much more reliant on each other's company. They then come to the uncomfortable realisation that they no longer have anything to offer each other and that their only link is their children. They may even begin to feel like strangers.

It takes courage to be able to walk away from a relationship, especially if this will cause ructions within the family. Yet what other choices are there?

the start of something new

The illustration on this card depicts a peculiar moon, which appears to be full and new at the same time. This indicates that one cycle has to end before another can begin. Full moons are a classic sign of endings, while new moons are traditional indications of fresh beginnings. So there is more hope contained within this card's message than may at first be apparent. There might also be a sense of relief, even if it seems in bad taste to admit it to yourself. Even though you are coping with the breakdown of the relationship and all that this involves, you may experience a dawning sense of liberation and excitement at what the next stage of your life may bring. You might also be able to salvage a good deal from the relationship, especially if you are able to end it at the right time. Clinging on in desperation long after you should have let go may only lead to bitterness and frustration on both sides.

Sometimes, the Eight of Cups describes the end of cherished hopes and dreams. You may have to accept that you gave a project your best shot and that it simply did not succeed, so it is time to move on to something else. There is no point in chastising yourself for this because you will have to accept that it is just one of those things. Later on, you may even decide that it was obviously not meant to happen, or you will realise that you are glad your plans had to be abandoned because something much better took their place.

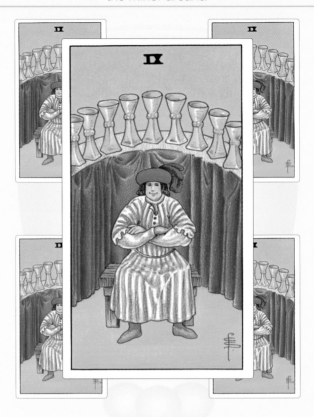

nine of cups

This card carries a great deal of promise. It suggests that you are about to realise a longed-for dream, or will soon have many reasons to feel happy. The Nine of Cups is the wish card of the Minor Arcana, so it is always a welcome sight in a spread because it indicates that everything will go your way and you will soon be sitting pretty.

The promise foretold by this card can manifest in many different ways. It might be the happiness that comes from a satisfying relationship, in which your emotional needs are met and you enjoy the sense of being united with your beloved. It could be the euphoria, excitement and anticipation that precede the birth of a child, with all the joyful preparations that accompany such an event. Sometimes the Nine of Cups highlights the potential for creative fulfilment that arises when you are about to complete a task in which you have invested a lot of time and energy. You are not yet at the point of celebrating the finished result but you are pretty confident that a successful end is within your grasp. It can also refer to a satisfying spiritual phase, when you feel at one with the universe and everyone around you. Or it may indicate the promise of financial prosperity, so you can look forward to being comfortably off and not having to worry about unexpected expenses.

contentment or complacency?

Although this is one of the most positive cards of the Minor Arcana, it carries a warning not to become complacent, nor to take your good fortune for granted. For example, if you are enjoying a very contented phase in a close relationship, the appearance of the Nine of Cups suggests that you may begin to think that you do not have to make much effort to sustain the partnership. You might observe other people's relationships coming apart at the seams and happily tell yourself that you will never need to worry about this happening to you. If you are experiencing an affluent financial period, you could develop a tendency to assume that things will always be this good. There is also a chance that you might want to ignore the plight of others less fortunate than yourself and even though you may be experiencing an abundant phase, you might not want to share your money or belongings with others. This is especially likely if the Four of Pentacles also appears in the spread, since this will emphasise the theme of being unwilling to take financial risks or to increase your outgoings.

a happy ending

If life has been difficult or you have been struggling to cope with severe problems, such as poor health or a tense period in a relationship, this card gives you the reassurance that the situation will soon improve. However, you should not assume that this will automatically happen without any effort on your part; you might then discover that the Nine of Cups sometimes promises more than it delivers. Nevertheless, if you play by the rules of this card you have good reason for looking forward to happier and more abundant times ahead.

ten of cups

This is one of the most joyful and optimistic of all the tarot cards because it symbolises the culmination of something that you have desired and brings a sense of completion and contentment, happiness and joy. The Ten of Cups indicates a feeling of achievement about something that means a great deal to you. It can describe a pleasant, peaceful family life in which everything is running smoothly and everyone is getting on well with everyone else. Your affection for each other continues to grow and deepen, so you are creating a stable family background in which you can all share. If you are about to move house when this card appears, it suggests that you will be extremely happy in your new home and you may devote much care and attention to it because you will want to make it your own.

finding the end of the rainbow

The illustration on this card shows a couple looking out at a lush landscape while a pair of children play happily beside them. A rainbow curves over their heads, hinting that they have found what they are looking for. In some way, this describes your situation; you have achieved something that is giving you pleasure and which is a cause for celebration.

Sometimes the card appears when you are moving out of a difficult phase into one that will be much easier and more comfortable. The problems you are undergoing may not have a fairytale ending but they will be resolved to everyone's benefit and you will begin to experience a much more peaceful period in your life. If you have been caught in the maelstrom of a family feud, or have been enduring one of those turbulent phases when arguments never seem far away, you can look forward to happier and more harmonious times.

This card describes a peaceful contentment, a sense of on-going happiness that is more muted than the euphoria described by the Nine of Cups. Nevertheless, it may be more dependable and permanent, especially if it refers to a tranquil family life.

a beacon of hope

The Ten of Cups is especially welcome in a spread if life has been treating you harshly recently or you have struggled through an illness. It reassures you that things will soon improve, and this more positive phase will continue for some time to come. Often, it can suggest a change of residence, even if you are not considering this at the time of the reading. You may soon be drawn to somewhere with a rural atmosphere or plenty of land, especially if the Empress or Four of Wands also appears in the spread. This move might even lead to the sort of happy family life that is illustrated on the card.

The card can also describe being comfortable in the knowledge that your life is progressing in a way that feels good, and that you are moving in the right direction. You are at home with yourself and have much to be grateful for.

PAGE of CUPS

page of cups

As with all the court cards, the Page of Cups can refer either to a situation or to a person. Yet the two may be connected in some way. For instance, the card might indicate a new relationship with someone who is described by the Page of Cups.

as a situation

When the card refers to a situation, it is one that has only just begun and which may therefore be very fragile. Perhaps you want to nurture it like a tender plant and not expose it to any harsh emotions for a while. In other words, you may be on your best behaviour! If this situation is a budding romance, the card suggests that it will continue to grow and develop, and will bring you emotional satisfaction. It may not turn out to be the biggest relationship of your life but it will be enjoyable. It might well grow into a strong, sustaining friendship rather than a romance, since Cups rule all personal relationships and do not simply represent love affairs.

There is also a possibility that the Page of Cups refers to a situation that will bring creative or spiritual benefits. One example might be embarking on a course or period of study that will teach you more about the world and increase your understanding of other people. The precise nature of the course is not as important as the effects that it will have on you, so it could be as diverse as a course in a complementary therapy or an accountancy class, provided it softens your approach to the world or makes you more accepting of the people around you. The Page of Cups might also describe the dawning of a strong religious conviction or philosophical belief that will sustain you and give you a great deal to think about; it may even offer you a new direction in life. This will be shown by the cards that surround the Page of Cups, especially if they are connected with change, such as the Wheel of Fortune or the World.

as a person

When the Page of Cups refers to a person, they are young. They may even be an adolescent. They are helpful, considerate and sensitive. You might feel that you can rely on their support, loyalty or sheer good nature. They may also be interested in creative or spiritual topics.

However, the very fact that they are described by a Page means that you do not know them very well. They may have only recently arrived in your life or could be in the process of leaving it. Perhaps they are really only an acquaintance at the time of the reading but you hope you will get to know them better. The nature of the Cups suit suggests that you will have some form of emotional contact with them; if you are a teacher, for instance, the Page may refer to one of your favourite students. Sometimes, the card describes someone who will never play a major role in your life but who will perhaps provide a service for you or help you to work towards a particular goal. They will have some significance for you, even if this is only at the time of the reading.

143

knight of cups

The Knight of Cups has two main meanings. It represents either a person or a situation. In either case, this is connected with your emotions, spirituality or anything else that has a great deal of meaning for you.

as a situation

Knights represent a situation that is busy and lively. Things may happen very fast or you could be caught up in a whirlwind of excitement about something. The Knight of Cups describes an enjoyable time that will engage you emotionally. You could become swept up in a creative or artistic venture into which you put your heart and soul, and which will bring you many different rewards. For example, in your spare time you might develop a new skill that you will grow to love and which will give you a tremendous amount of pleasure and satisfaction. It will provide fresh meaning to your life.

Sometimes, the Knight of Cups indicates that you will be presented with a wonderful opportunity. This might involve travel, especially if you will be crossing a stretch of water or visiting somewhere hot or dry. Occasionally, the card may suggest that you will soon move house to a place where you will be very content. This is especially likely if the Four of Wands, Empress or Ten of Pentacles also appear in the reading. Alternatively, you may be given the chance to develop your intuition or healing skills, whether you do so informally or are taught by someone who has the experience you need.

If you are toying with the idea of following a new path in life, or finally doing something that you have always promised yourself you will try, the Knight of Cups gives you a great deal of encouragement. It is telling you to follow your heart and do what will make you happy.

as a person

When the Knight of Cups refers to a person, it can be a man or a woman. They are not very important to you at the time of the reading, although your affection for them could wax or wane with time. For example, the card may represent someone you are currently getting to know or who will always be on the periphery of your life. Alternatively, they might be someone who once meant a lot to you but who is no longer so important. They are fairly young: they might be in their late teens or twenties.

The person represented by the Knight of Cups is idealistic, friendly and creative. They are fun to be around and they may be very good for your ego. For instance, they might flatter you or you could become caught up in a heady romance with them. If you fall in love with them, in its early stages your relationship will be delightfully enjoyable. It may even seem too good to be true, and you may both be slightly in love with the idea of love. At this point in your relationship, you are completely intoxicated with one another. All the tensions and challenges of a long-term relationship will come later.

queen of cups

As its name suggests, the Queen of Cups denotes a mature woman who is important to you in some way at the time of the reading. Sometimes, however, this card will encourage you to express some of the personality traits that belong to the Queen of Cups.

the earth mother

The Queen of Cups is the classic earth mother. She has strong maternal instincts and is sensitive, considerate and emotional. This is the sort of person who tucks lame ducks under her wing and who is concerned about other people's welfare. She may well have a large and loving family, perhaps including several children and pets, or she has developed an extended family of cherished friends. She is probably a skilled homemaker, with a strong flair for making a place feel safe and cosy and is an excellent cook, although her food is more

146

likely to be traditional and satisfying than to belong to the cutting edge of gastronomic fashion. The Queen of Cups may not be particularly concerned about her appearance because she has little time to devote to it, or considers that it is the person inside who matters.

The woman described by this card is intuitive, possibly even psychic. She may give the impression of being tuned into the currents of energy flowing around her, and being in touch with the hidden elements of the universe. She might also practise some form of healing, work as a counsellor or psychotherapist, or be a musician, poet or artist.

Although the woman indicated by the Queen of Cups is so sensitive and emotional, nevertheless there is a part of her that she always keeps separate. You may feel that you will never know one aspect of her personality because it seems out of reach and untouchable. Perhaps she is so otherworldly that she can appear quite distant and detached at times. You may feel that you cannot get to know her as you would like because she has so many other claims on her time, with so many people to care for. You may not want to intrude.

a psychic sponge

The woman indicated by the Queen of Cups is extremely sensitive to what is going on around her. As a result, her emotions may ebb and flow like the tides, according to what she is experiencing at the time. She may have to be careful about the company she keeps, not spending too long with people who are draining, negative or very angry, because she has a tendency to absorb such emotions like a sponge. Like all very sensitive people, it is vitally important that the woman represented by the Queen of Cups is fully grounded. This will involve practising simple grounding exercises, such as imagining that roots are growing out of the soles of her feet and anchoring her to the centre of the earth. She may also benefit from plenty of physical exercise since this is another excellent way to keep in touch with earthly energy and not spend too much time in other realms.

KING of CUPS

king of cups

The King of Cups describes a mature man who is important to you at the time of the reading. Alternatively, the card may describe certain personality traits that you should develop within yourself.

a figure of authority

If the King of Cups describes someone you know, this man may already occupy a central place in your life or perhaps he will soon do so. He has some form of authority and is probably widely respected. He is friendly and helpful, although he is not as approachable as you might like. You may get the impression that he always holds some part of himself in reserve, perhaps through self-defence.

Very often the King of Cups describes someone who works in an advisory capacity. He may practise some form of counselling, so he provides emotional or psychological support. If you are his client, he will necessarily have to remain slightly detached for professional reasons. Alternatively, he might be a businessman who is in charge of a lot of people and sometimes, the King of Cups acts as a mentor, perhaps working as an inspirational teacher or lecturer. His job may also bring him into contact with children. For instance, he might be a doctor or nurse who specialises in paediatrics, or he could even be a foster father.

Cups is the suit connected with spirituality and religion, so the King of Cups might have some form of spiritual authority. For example, he could be the minister of a church or the highly respected teacher of a belief or philosophy. Despite his outwardly friendly demeanour, he may have to keep people at arm's length to avoid being completely subsumed by their emotional demands and their expectations of him.

Given his creative and artistic abilities, the King of Cups may have an important job in the world of the media, advertising or the arts. He is probably successful and accomplished, although once again he may not be renowned for his friendliness. He has strong instincts that he uses well and is probably highly intuitive, which helps him to tune into the latest business trends or creative movements. Sometimes, he may appear to take risks because he prefers to trust his gut instincts rather than the results of focus groups or market research.

opening up emotionally

When the tarot recommends that you learn from the personality traits of the King of Cups, it is highly likely that you are being told to become more demonstrative and emotional. If you have been keeping your feelings to yourself, this is the time to open up to people you trust. You need to develop your feminine side, whether you are a man or a woman.

swords

ACE of SWORDS

ace of swords

This card indicates the birth of an idea, project or relationship that will be engrossing and fascinating. It may be difficult to stop thinking about it because it has such a powerful effect on you. It might also seem to be the answer to current problems or the solution to a difficult question that has been perplexing you for some time. The Ace of Swords can also herald powerful changes that may seem to have karmic connections or be linked with your destiny.

decisions, decisions

Sometimes the Ace of Swords describes the need to reach a tough decision about something. This will involve being able to view the situation as objectively and dispassionately as possible, given the circumstances. There is no room for sentiment with this suit, so you may have to harden your heart about something or do your best to put emotional considerations to one side. You might even have to be cruel to be kind. However, once you have made up your mind, it is highly likely that you will be resolute and unwilling to contemplate any other option. It will be a relief finally to have reached a solution and to be able to stand by it.

When in the process of coming to any sort of decision, the Ace of Swords is reminding you to think it through very carefully. This should be relatively easy since your mind will keep straying to this subject, but even so you must be sure to examine it from as many angles as possible and you might want to take expert advice or discuss it with people you trust. Your thought processes will be very clear, incisive and constructive.

There is an uncompromising quality to the Ace of Swords, which will be helpful if you are in a situation in which you need to stand up for yourself or defend your opinions. You may have to be very certain about this, even if it goes against the grain or you are not used to taking such a definite stance. You must stick to the facts rather than allow yourself to be sidetracked by sentiment. Nevertheless, it is important to be aware of the way you are behaving, and not to sound so firm, dogmatic or dictatorial that you arouse someone's opposition for no good reason or do yourself more harm than good. For instance, if you are involved in a legal dispute, the Ace of Swords may be telling you that the outcome will be favourable if you act in an honourable fashion.

powerful emotions

When describing your emotional state, the Ace of Swords shows that you are very wrapped up in your feelings. You may be in the grip of some powerful, intense emotions which are difficult to handle with any degree of insouciance. You are experiencing your emotions on a very profound level, whether you are happy about something or in the depths of despair. If the process of falling in love is described by this card, it shows that the situation is likely to have a transformational effect on you.

151

two of swords

This is a difficult card because it shows that you are stuck in an unpleasant situation through fear or a reluctance to acknowledge what is happening to you. However, things can be changed if you are prepared to face up to what is going on around you, and to recognise your fears for what they are. Until that happens, you are likely to remain at an impasse.

Sometimes, the Two of Swords indicates a brief respite from a difficult problem, in which you are able to maintain an uneasy truce while knowing that more trouble is probably on the way.

caught in a stalemate

The illustration on this card shows a blindfolded woman sitting in front of a rocky sea. She clasps a sword in each hand, with her arms crossed over her chest. The swords are finely balanced in the air, and it must take a great deal of effort to keep them in that position. Her feet are planted firmly on the ground, showing that she is not moving from her seat. This emphasises the central meaning of the Two of Swords, which is that fear of examining your current situation renders you unable to do anything about it. You may be exerting a great deal of emotional and mental energy in maintaining the status quo because you are too scared to alter it. Making changes would involve accepting what is happening to you, and this may seem too threatening for you at the moment.

Swords rule fears, worries and other mental difficulties, so there is a chance that the situation is not nearly as fraught, dangerous or impossible as you imagine. You might be building it up in your mind so it assumes mammoth proportions. For instance, you may be very worried about a problem you are experiencing in a relationship. You are struggling to communicate with your partner, or you could be at daggers drawn for most of the time. As the situation deteriorates, you could begin to fear that your partner wants to leave you or is having an affair. Such worries build up in your mind yet you are unable to discuss them with your partner because you are terrified that he or she will confirm your worst fears. As a result, you are locked in a fearful state of mind because you do not want to know the truth, yet until you do know it you are powerless to take any action.

The same type of stalemate might apply if you are worried about your health but frightened to seek medical advice because of what this might lead to. Yet, at the same time, you know that you will not be able to rest until you have taken the very action that you fear.

a peaceful interlude

If you are caught in the middle of a dispute, an unpleasant legal case or a long-running argument with someone, the Two of Swords can indicate a short interlude in which you are able to take a breather and regroup. This will enable you to gather your strength and harness mental resources for the next skirmish.

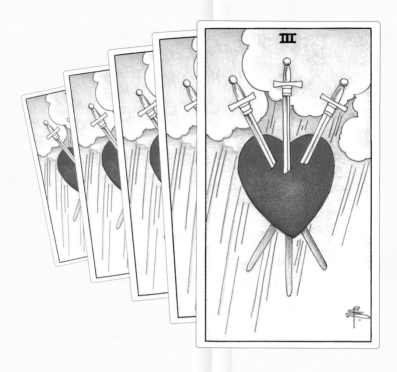

three of swords

This is not an easy card at all since it describes heartfelt worries, disappointment, difficulties and separation. There may even be some form of deception or treachery that must be endured, because the Three of Swords often appears when people are involved in eternal triangles. It indicates a poignant, unhappy and even agonising time during which you go through emotional extremes and feel as though you have reached rock bottom.

talking things through

The nature of the Swords suit is very telling here. It describes worries and adversity, but it may suggest that you are allowing the problem to get out of proportion. Sometimes this card refers to a medical procedure, such as an operation, that is a cause for anxiety. Some part of you might even be secretly enjoying the drama of the situation, especially if you are receiving plenty of sympathy as a result of it. This is entirely natural but it may not be helping you to solve the dilemma. Alternatively, you might have to cope with someone else who is busy milking the problem of every drop of melodrama they can squeeze out of it.

Whether you are actively involved in the situation or can only stand on the sidelines as an observer, it is very important to discuss your feelings and to share them with everyone else. Honest, open and straightforward communication is the best way to deal with what is happening. Swords describe the importance of talking to others, and such conversations will provide you with a safety valve. You might want to confide in friends or may prefer to talk to a professional counsellor. It could also help to put your feelings down in writing, perhaps in a journal, especially if you do not know who you can trust or you are reluctant to make the problem public.

separation

The Three of Swords also describes separation. A close relationship may come to an end, leaving you feeling bereft and emotionally dislocated. You might even feel as though you have been deserted by loved ones and left to cope on your own. Perhaps the rift in your relationship has caused people to take sides and you feel isolated as a result. This is a miserable state of affairs and it may be that all you can do is grit your teeth and get through it. Learn from the experience and do your best to resist the temptation to be vengeful, cruel or spiteful. Such attitudes will not help the situation, even if they make you feel better for a brief spell, and they are likely to come back to haunt you. Instead, you will gain inner strength and comfort from knowing that you are behaving as well as you can under the circumstances.

The separation might not be permanent: it may occur because one partner lives a long way away from the other, or because their job takes them far afield. If so, the temporary absence of your partner could bring you closer together or encourage you to develop your own emotional resources so you become less dependent on them. This will strengthen your relationship because you will feel more confident within yourself.

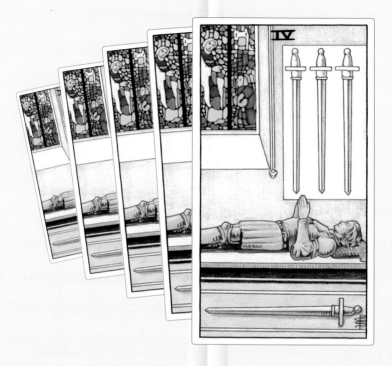

four of swords

This card advocates taking a rest and retiring from the fray for a while. This might be because you have reached the end of your emotional or mental resources for the time being and you need to recuperate. Very often, the card appears in a spread after a period of hard work, showing that it is time to recharge your batteries before embarking on the next phase of exertion and effort.

hang up your swords

The illustration on this card shows a stone effigy on a church tomb. Three swords are suspended from the wall behind the effigy while the fourth lies along the bottom of the tomb. However, a church is a place of sanctuary, where no swords should be used. In the past, when men carried swords as a matter of course, they always blunted the points of their blades on the outside wall of the church before entering it. This card therefore carries a clear message that you must relinquish your own swords for the time being. But what does this all mean? In the tarot, the suit of Swords represents all mental activities, such as thoughts, negotiations, worries and decisions, and actions that result from mental activities, such as writing. It also rules discord, strife and problems. The Four of Swords is therefore telling you to relax and suspend such activities for a short while.

Instead of being active, you need to reflect, rest and recover. If you have been wearing yourself out with a great deal of hard work or some taxing mental activity, you need a break before you can continue. Perhaps you feel as though your mental abilities have become blunted for the time being through exhaustion or over-work. If you are worried about something, you may have reached the point where your thoughts are simply going round and round your head until you cannot think straight.

calling a truce

If you have been involved in some form of acrimony, dispute or even a vendetta with someone, the Four of Swords is telling you to call a truce for the time being and not take things any further. This will give you the chance to rethink the situation and it may also prevent it becoming any worse. For instance, if you are considering taking legal action against someone and you draw this card, it is urging you to think long and hard about your options before proceeding. You may realise that you have nothing to gain from legal action, or that it is not worth the trouble it will cause. Perhaps it seems too drastic a step or you have no wish to prolong the dispute any further.

By taking a step back, you may be able to take some time for reflection and contemplation. You could become interested in meditation, perhaps setting aside time for it each day. You might even decide to take part in a retreat that allows you to withdraw from the stresses of daily life for a short while, so you can think things through and gain a better perspective of them.

five of swords

Something has not worked out and it is time to accept defeat, or at the very least to acknowledge that the experience has not been a complete success. Although you have gained in some ways, you have lost in others. You could even feel uncomfortable about the outcome or about the part that you played in the situation.

This is not an easy card by any means, although it is not as difficult as some of its fellow members of the Swords suit. Very often, it indicates the painful results of a disagreement with someone. You may feel that you overstepped the mark in some way, perhaps by saying things that should have remained unspoken. Although this felt good at the time, or you lost your self-control and were unable to stop yourself saying something hurtful, you might now feel ashamed of yourself or wish that you could put back the clock and do things differently. If you usually have quite a high opinion of

158

yourself, or hope that others respect you, you might have to accept that your image has been tarnished in some way or that you have shown yourself to be human after all. This loss of face may be hard to tolerate, yet it could teach you some valuable lessons about yourself.

triumphing over others

The Five of Swords can also describe triumphing over other people, but not in a particularly pleasant way. There may be something sneaky or underhand about how it was done, perhaps because it was not an evenly matched contest or someone used unfair tactics in order to get what they wanted. It might even turn out to be a pyrrhic victory, in which the cost of winning is too great and it outweighs the feelings of success. For instance, if the card refers to a legal case, it might be one in which the victor manipulates their evidence to blacken the reputation of their adversary. They may win the case as a result, but their conscience will nag them. Alternatively, they might be vilified by others for not having behaved honourably. There is also the possibility of unpleasant gossip with this card. Someone could spread damaging rumours or make very barbed comments that hurt another person's reputation or cast doubts about their probity.

moving on

Every tarot card can teach us a lesson, and it can also offer us encouragement. The Five of Swords, despite its uncomfortable messages and associations, persuades us to reconcile ourselves with the disagreeable events that have taken place and to move on from them. The incidents described by the Five of Swords may even act as a catalyst, introducing change that leads to new horizons and less problematic situations in the future. The card is especially encouraging if it is accompanied by the Wheel of Fortune, which indicates a change in fortune, or any of the Aces, since these speak of new beginnings. The period of time illustrated by the Five of Swords may be grim but it will not last forever.

six of swords

This card describes moving away from an unpleasant experience into calmer waters. However, it may not feel like this at the time, perhaps because you are still feeling very battered by what has happened or you dare not allow yourself to hope that the situation will improve because you do not want to be disappointed if things fail to turn out well.

feeling beleaguered

The illustration here shows a cloaked figure, accompanied by a small child, sitting in a wooden boat. Behind them, a man is using a punt to steer them across a stretch of water to the land that lies opposite. The water to the right of the boat is choppy but the water to the left looks calm. The cloaked figure is hunched and radiates a sense of defeat and resignation. Six swords surround the adult and child, increasing the feeling of dejection and of being hemmed in by problems. Although the passengers may be moving away from distress and into a better future, the cloaked figure seems braced for further trouble.

The Six of Swords therefore describes a feeling of being beleaguered by problems and of being unable to escape them. Even if logic tells you that a difficult period is now at an end and you can put it behind you, you could be plagued by the memory of it and by the fear that it will happen again. Your mind may keep replaying the experience, so you are unable to forget it, and you might be unable to sleep because of it, especially if this card is accompanied by the Nine of Swords. However, it is likely that your fears are unfounded and it may help to discuss the situation with someone you trust, because the very act of explaining your fears may help to put them into perspective. Your confident might be a friend or you could prefer to talk to a trained counsellor or psychotherapist.

taking time off

The Six of Swords often describes the need to take a holiday, especially if life has become very fraught or you are exhausted. You may not even realise how necessary it is that you have a break, and you might tell yourself that you are too busy to go away or that it is a waste of money. However, once you are on holiday you will understand that it was exactly what you needed. You will begin to think more clearly and will feel rejuvenated. Then when you return, you will feel better equipped to deal with life with renewed zest and enthusiasm.

on the move

If this card appears when you are having difficulties with neighbours or other people in your local surroundings, it may be encouraging you to move home. This might be the obvious answer and one which you feel is necessary, or it may simply be an easier solution than staying put and enduring your current problems any longer.

seven of swords

This is a difficult card because it describes the need to tread carefully in order to emerge successfully from a situation. There may be an element of subterfuge associated with this, in which you have to play your cards very close to your chest or act in what might seem to be an underhand manner. Alternatively, of course, you may find yourself having to deal with someone who behaves towards *you* in this way and who therefore makes you feel cheated or short-changed.

the need for evasion

There are times when it is necessary to be evasive or economical with the truth, even though you may not like yourself for it, and the presence of the Seven of Swords in a spread suggests that such an occasion has now arisen. Although your instincts may be to tell someone the truth or to be completely open with them, this card is hinting that it might not be such a good idea.

There are many reasons for this, of course. It could be that nothing will be gained from being brutally honest with this person and that it would be much better to give them an edited version of the truth. You might even hurt them in some way by giving them all the facts. Alternatively, you may have to keep certain things to yourself as a means of self-protection because the truth would cause so much disruption or trouble. For instance, you may be giving your partner snippets of information about something at carefully chosen intervals, so they can get used to it, rather than drop a bombshell that completely devastates them or leads to an almighty row.

Nevertheless, even though there may be occasions when it is politic to massage the facts or only tell half the story, there are others when this is not such a good idea. The Seven of Swords carries a warning not to be underhand or dishonest simply because it is easier than telling the truth. Nor should you deliberately trick or deceive anyone in order to profit financially. Swords are double-edged and you will inevitably experience some form of retribution sooner or later.

the need to be on your guard

You should be very careful if you are involved in a legal dispute when this card appears. It may be warning you that someone will be dishonest or use some form of trickery to win the case. Rather like a magician, the other person could try to use misdirection to deflect attention from something they want to hide.

All forms of theft are suggested by the Seven of Swords, so you may want to take extra care of your belongings when this card appears. Remember, however, that not all theft is materialistic; people steal in many ways, and you might encounter someone who tries to extract information from you by asking impertinent or probing questions, or who does their best to steal your peace of mind by making you overly worried about something. Naturally, you should also guard against doing such things yourself.

eight of swords

This card describes being trapped and restricted by one's own fears. These can be so strong that it seems almost impossible to get beyond them. Swords represent thoughts, and in this case your thoughts have become a prison from which it is difficult to break free. Yet escape is not impossible by any means, as you will discover when you are able to find the courage to assess your situation.

facing up to your fears

The illustration on this card shows a woman standing on boggy, wet ground. She is blindfolded and her arms are bound to her sides. She is hemmed in by eight swords, although they do not completely surround her. The swords in the illustration represent the power of your mind to frighten you and make you feel trapped. Some of your fears may be entirely justified, but you might have allowed them to assume monumental proportions or to place immense restrictions on your life. For instance, this card is an apt description of someone who has been so badly hurt by lovers in the past that they have chosen to cut themselves off emotionally so there is no risk of history repeating itself. They want to remain untouched and unaffected by what they perceive to be the dangers of relationships, yet they miss so many joys in the process. They have also left themselves little room for manoeuvre.

Sometimes the Eight of Swords describes someone who has had restrictions imposed on them by someone else. They might have a very rigid parent, or a domineering partner, who refuses to let them have a life of their own and who has turned them into a virtual captive. If you find yourself in this sort of situation it will take guts and courage to break free, and this could seem an impossible task because you are so scared of what the other person will do if you go against their will. You may need the loving support of friends or family, or even professional help, in order to find the strength to do this.

This card can also describe someone who feels trapped in a dead relationship. They may be doing their best to persuade themselves otherwise, and are unwilling to see the situation for what it is. Yet until they can accept the facts and see what is happening to them, they will be unable to do anything about the problem, nor to move on from it.

cutting loose

If you find that you are stuck in a trap of your own making, and feel hemmed in by worries or fears, once you have summoned up your courage to address the problem you may find that it is easier to solve than you realised. If you are prepared to take off your self-imposed blindfold and to see the situation in its true light, you will understand that there is a way out of it. You could even find that somehow you were blocking your own exit route. Solutions that you were oblivious to before may now present themselves with clarity, making you wonder why they did not occur to you in the past.

nine of swords

This is one of the most miserable cards of the entire tarot deck because it speaks of despair, severe anxiety and desperation. It describes a state of abject misery, when we feel hag-ridden by worries and at the end of our tether. There is a feeling of impending doom, that everything is about to crash down about our ears and that our worst fears will be realised. Sometimes, it describes the aftermath of disaster, and the ghastly knowledge that something terrible has happened and we have to find some way to cope with it.

always darkest before the dawn

One of the classic meanings of the Nine of Swords is 'sleepless nights'. The illustration on the card confirms this, as it shows a woman sitting up in bed, her face buried in her hands and nine swords hanging on the wall above her. It can therefore describe the sense of desperation that accompanies severe worries. You might be in a situation where you feel full of doom and gloom, convinced that the worst is about to happen. Your prospects may seem very bleak, so it is tempting to believe that nothing will go right or even that things will go from bad to worse. Whether or not this is true is another matter.

The Nine of Swords can therefore describe the tendency to believe that your situation is much worse than it really is. Your imagination may be spinning out of control, creating terrifying scenarios based on 'what if' questions that have little or no bearing on reality. What if you lose your job? What if your partner then leaves you? What if this means you can no longer afford to live in your present home? What if you then become homeless? Your mind continues to create ghastly pictures that increase your anxiety levels until you feel completely desolate and helpless.

bereavement and loss

Sometimes there is the reassurance that the feared situation described by the Nine of Swords has not yet happened and may never do so. However, this card can also describe the grief and desolation that follows a bereavement or some other form of crisis, when one is only too aware of what has happened. A relationship may have ended, a loved one might have died or a serious illness could have been diagnosed. How can you get through this?

being able to cope

The card carries the encouragement that you will eventually find ways to manage your predicament. Even if you cannot find a magic solution to all your problems in one fell swoop, it will help to take things one day at a time. If your imagination is working overtime, you may be able to stop your mind conjuring up such dreadful images and you could find the emotional and mental strength to begin to take charge of your thoughts and of your situation. You might even be able to fight back, and to begin the healing process. As with all the Swords, it might also be wise to talk about what is wrong and to seek professional help.

ten of swords

There is a ghastly sense of finality about this card. Your worst suspicions have been realised and circumstances have left you feeling completely demolished, as though you have been slain. This could be as a result of a betrayal, making you feel that you have been stabbed in the back, or it may seem that the odds are stacked against you and you will inevitably be defeated in what you are trying to achieve.

the end of something

The Ten of Swords is a card of endings, and it often indicates the termination of a particular phase in a relationship. However, it may not be the end of the relationship itself, since this might be transformed as a result of the events described by the card. When you draw this card, it is important to remember that although it represents life at its most bleak, it also indicates a turning point. You have hit rock bottom, so the only direction in which you can now go is up. The illustration on the card shows a jet black sky that lightens towards the horizon, indicating the dawn of another day. This is telling you to gain hope from the future.

playing the victim

The card shows a figure lying face down, with ten swords protruding from its back. The implication is that these wounds have been inflicted by someone else, hence the sense of victimisation that often accompanies the circumstances described by this card. You may feel outrage, asking how someone has dared to do this to you. There is something very potent about the idea of being stabbed in the back, with its suggestion that you could not see your attacker advancing towards you and they therefore had the advantage of stealth or surprise. It seems unfair, although in some situations stabbing one's opponent in the back may be the only way to save one's own life.

asking some important questions

It is therefore very tempting to assign all the blame for the situation on the other person, and to tell yourself that you are the innocent party. However, you will learn most from the experience – and help to ensure that you do not have to repeat it – if you can view it objectively. This may involve asking yourself questions that are uncomfortable but which nevertheless need answers. How have you contributed to the current state of this situation? Have you ignored warning signs that something is wrong in the hope that everything would resolve itself without any effort on your part? Have you colluded with your partner in some way? Does the relationship stir up painful childhood memories that reinforce your worst fears about being unlovable or abandoned? Were you metaphorically stabbed in the back because that was the only way the other person felt safe enough to confront you? Until you feel able even to attempt to answer these questions honestly, the magnitude of the dilemma will be a barrier that stops you from moving on, just as the swords form an impenetrable line down the person's back.

PAGE of SWORDS

page of swords

The Page of Swords can refer either to a situation or to a person. It shows the dawning of intellectual ideas and the arrival of news. The nature of the surrounding cards will reveal whether this is positive or negative.

as a situation

When the card refers to a situation, it is one that is in its early stages. Swords represent everything connected with communication and information, so it is highly likely that the Page of Swords heralds some news that will soon reach you. Whether you will like what you hear depends on the nature of the surrounding cards, so examine them carefully. This card can also denote the beginnings of a negotiation or legal suit in which you will have to be on your mettle. You will also need to draw on your diplomatic skills, since words will have to be used with care and thought. If you are expected to make a decision when the Page of Swords appears, it is telling you to think things through very carefully and not rush into any hasty judgements.

Sometimes, the Page of Swords refers to an agreement or contract that must be signed. If so, you should read it through very carefully, concentrating on the small print, in case it contains clauses that might catch the unwary or accidental mistakes that will cause problems later on. If the card is accompanied by the King of Swords, you may decide to consult an expert before committing yourself to anything, such as asking a lawyer to read through a contract before you are prepared to sign it.

The Page of Swords can also describe the beginnings of an intellectual pursuit that will really stretch your mind, such as a university course. On a less ambitious level, it can refer to an enjoyment of puzzles, competitions, chess games and other mental challenges.

as a person

When referring to a person, the Page of Swords describes someone who is probably a child or adolescent. Alternatively, they can be someone who is in touch with you at a distance, such as a friend who lives abroad or someone you communicate with over the Internet. You do not necessarily know them very well, perhaps because they are on the periphery of your life or they are simply conveying news to you.

Whoever this person is, they are clever, opinionated and very good with words. They may be slightly too clever for your liking, and you might suspect they are capable of sharp practice or deception. For instance, this could be a fast-talking salesperson who convinces you to buy something that you do not really need or want. The card can also describe someone who is spreading gossip or rumours, or who is manipulative and should therefore be treated with caution and wariness.

knight of swords

The Knight of Swords has two main meanings. It can represent either a situation or a person. In each case, it is connected with hasty and rapid action, and with decisions that are taken very quickly.

as a situation

Something is about to happen very quickly when the Knight of Swords appears. It may even be the sort of occurrence that leaves you reeling when it is all over and you have time to think about it properly. You might wonder what on earth possessed you to take the action you did, or you may realise that your life has changed radically as a result. At the time, you are so busy keeping up with everything that is going on that you have little or no chance to analyse what is happening to you. At its most typical, the Knight of Swords describes a situation that begins very quickly, sweeps you

172

along at a headlong pace and then ends just as rapidly. The nature of this will be described by the surrounding cards, but if it is accompanied by the Wheel of Fortune, Death or the Tower, it will be a dramatic change that has a powerful impact on your life. If it is accompanied by the Four of Wands, the Empress or the Ten of Cups, it could indicate a sudden change of residence.

The Knight of Swords can also describe a situation for which you need to muster strength of purpose, bravery and heroism in order to endure it. Although this may be difficult, ultimately you will succeed unless the surrounding cards say otherwise. You may have to behave like a warrior going into battle in order to do this, and you will be able to rise to the challenge. This is not a faint-hearted card! Instead, it speaks of the need to throw yourself into a situation and to act in whichever way is required of you, especially if that means toughing something out or digging deep inside yourself to discover the hero or heroine who lurks within. Life can seem like an epic adventure in this sort of situation, and when the dust has settled you may look back on the whole thing and wonder how on earth you managed to cope. Yet cope you did.

as a person

When the Knight of Swords refers to a person, they can be a young man or woman. They might not be very important to you when you have the reading, although your feelings for them may increase or decrease in time. For instance, you may have only just met them or, on the other hand, they could be leaving your life for some reason.

This person is successful, clever and quick-witted. They are also notable for their restlessness, impatience and their determination to make things happen, sometimes against their own better judgement. This is a person who rushes headlong into things without thinking them through carefully. They are also very assertive and can be quite a bully when they want to get their own way. You feel invincible when this individual is on your side, but overpowered when they are acting against you.

queen of swords

The Queen of Swords describes a mature woman who is important to you at the time of the reading. Alternatively, the card is encouraging you to express some of the personality traits that belong to the Queen of Swords.

going it alone

The Queen of Swords often represents a woman who has suffered and whose attitude to life has been coloured accordingly. Traditionally, she is a widow or divorcée who has come to terms with being alone, and who has known many privations and much sadness. Very often, she lives alone and is extremely self-reliant. The woman denoted by the Queen of Swords does not like asking for help because she prides herself on being self-sufficient. She may also be wary of putting herself in a position where she owes other people favours.

She is practical and intelligent, qualities which she might use professionally. For instance, she may be involved in social work, the legal system or the teaching profession, or any other job in which she gives people advice. She does her best to be as accurate and well-informed as possible, and pays a great deal of attention to detail. When voicing her opinions, she is forthright and uncompromising.

Very often, this woman is powerful, which could be as a result of her influential career or she might simply have tremendous personal authority which shines through in everything she does. She is highly respected but it can be difficult to get to know her well, because she puts up such a strong emotional defence. For instance, she might hold forth stridently on politics or capital punishment, but be very reluctant to talk about her feelings or her private life.

Sometimes, the Queen of Swords represents a woman who is very enigmatic. She has such a complex personality that it is almost impossible to penetrate it. She can also be a fantasy figure in someone's life; a woman who is yearned for and adored, but who is too aloof to get involved in flesh and blood relationships as this would reduce her mystique and possibly make her vulnerable to emotional pain.

becoming more stoical

When the tarot encourages you to emulate the Queen of Swords' behaviour, very often it is her stoicism that is most pertinent. If you have been going through a hard time, it may help to adopt some of her resolve and ability to look adversity in the face. Perhaps your only option is to deal with what is happening to you in as logical and intelligent a way as possible.

Alternatively, if you are involved in a messy relationship with someone, the Queen of Swords may be encouraging you to gain some emotional distance and not to be so caught up in the other person. Perhaps you should withdraw emotionally or physically for a while.

KING of SWORDS

king of swords

The King of Swords describes a mature man who is important to you at the time of the reading. Alternatively, the card describes certain personality traits that you should develop within yourself.

an intellectual heavyweight

The man represented by the King of Swords is no fool. He is intelligent, witty, articulate and he thoroughly enjoys using his brain. His conversation is influenced by logic rather than emotion, and he likes to stick to the facts rather than get carried away by the power of his imagination. He needs plenty of mental stimulation to keep him amused, and he finds it very difficult to get on well with people who are sensitive or intuitive because they simply do not understand one another.

Very often, this man tends to be argumentative. He enjoys pitting his wits against those of others, and he is quick to point out their mistakes. He likes getting involved in logical disagreements and does not take them personally, although other people might. It is natural for him to demonstrate his intelligence at every opportunity.

No matter what he does for a living, this man radiates power and authority. Sometimes, his assertiveness makes him appear to be domineering and overweening, although he would probably be surprised at such a description. Occasionally, however, the King of Swords portrays a man who is a relentless bully and who abuses his position in order to gain control over others.

a professional adviser

One of the traditional meanings of this card is the individual who offers you guidance. So, when the King of Swords appears in a reading, it may be a suggestion that you should consult someone for their expert advice. This person is almost bound to be a professional, such as a lawyer, doctor, psychiatrist or priest. They will give you their honest and considered opinion, although you may not want to hear it because it makes uncomfortable listening.

friend or foe?

The man described by the King of Swords is a good friend but an implacable enemy. You would not want to cross him. The surrounding cards in the spread will give you more information about this, showing how friendly he will be to you. If he is supportive, he will be invaluable in a crisis because he can keep his head and maintain an objective viewpoint about what is happening. You may also be encouraged to do the same when you draw this card, and to pull back slightly from the situation so you are in a better position to analyse and judge it. Use your intelligence to assess your circumstances, and do your best to emulate the cool head and logical reasoning of the King of Swords.

sample readings

the celtic cross spread

This is a classic tarot spread and one that most people are familiar with. It is especially useful for gaining an overview of a situation because it explores it in such detail, allowing you to examine both the present and the past. You will find variations in the ways in which the cards are laid out, but the essential pattern of the spread always remains the same.

It is often a good spread to begin with, and you can then develop the reading with further spreads if necessary. Alternatively, the Celtic Cross may answer all your questions so there is no need to ask any more.

Simon came to see me at a very difficult point in his relationship with his boyfriend, Steve. He had just discovered that Steve was having an affair with their next-door neighbour. As if that were not bad enough, the neighbour was a woman, making Simon feel doubly betrayed. He said he felt as though he had been 'knifed through the heart'. He did not know what to do and wanted to consult the tarot for advice. Although he doubted that the affair would last long, he felt extremely hurt and could not decide whether to stay with Steve. He admitted that financial considerations also had a part to play in his decision since he did not want to have to sell their house, split the proceeds and buy a much smaller property with his share of the money. At the age of fifty-three, he felt he was too old to start again from scratch. Yet he was seething with anger and did not want to stay in what might be a doomed relationship purely for materialistic reasons. What should he do?

Not surprisingly, given the rawness of Simon's emotional state and the drama of the situation, the spread contained some difficult cards. Fortunately, there were only two Major Arcana cards, which suggested that matters were within Simon's hands rather than being controlled by outside forces.

When counting up the Minor Arcana suits, there were four Wands cards, indicating that there would be an element of risk-taking and intuition involved in Simon's ultimate decision.

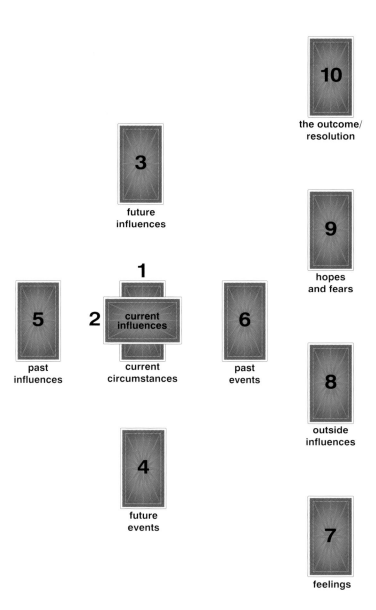

10

the outcome/
resolution

3

future
influences

9

hopes
and fears

1

5   **2** current
influences   **6**

past
influences

current
circumstances

past
events

8

outside
influences

4

future
events

7

feelings

3
future influences
Ace of Cups

1
current circumstances
The Tower

2
current influences
Five of Wands

5
past influences
Five of Pentacles

4
future events
The World

1 Current circumstances The Tower

This was a very apt card to describe Simon's current circumstances, since it showed that his world had crashed down around his ears, leading to loss of face. The Tower often indicates that a difficult situation has been gradually building up, although the crisis point can seemingly arrive out of the blue. Simon admitted that things had been difficult in his relationship with Steve for some time.

10
the outcome/resolution
Two of Wands

9
hopes and fears
Eight of Wands

6
past events
Three of Swords

8
outside influences
King of Wands

7
feelings
King of Swords

2 Current influences Five of Wands

The Five of Wands describes a difficult phase in which one has to struggle against all sorts of obstacles; nothing seems to go right. Life feels like a constant battle, and Simon admitted that it was not only his relationship with Steve that was causing problems. He was having difficulties at work, too, and even some of his household appliances were letting him down by going on the blink.

3 **Future influences** Ace of Cups

At least the future looks more encouraging. In fact, this is a very welcome harbinger of better times to come. The Ace of Cups is a classic indication of a new relationship or a satisfying phase in an existing partnership. So Simon and Steve may be able to weather their current storms and eventually make their relationship stronger. This card can also describe the start of a very creative or spiritual project that will bring much happiness and joy.

4 **Future events** The World

This very positive card echoes the encouragement given by the Ace of Cups, telling Simon that things will work out for him one way or the other. It shows the end of one cycle and the start of something new, so it might refer to the end of this difficult phase and the beginning of happier times. But it seems to be saying more than this and encouraging Simon to widen his horizons in some way, especially through travel or knowledge.

5 **Past influences** Five of Pentacles

Thankfully, this miserable card refers to the past, showing that at one point Simon was so wrapped up in one area of his life that he was in danger of losing something precious. He accepted that he had a very demanding job and in the past it had often interfered with his social life and also his health. This had been a bone of contention between him and Steve.

6 **Past events** Three of Swords

Never an easy card, here the Three of Swords describes Simon's anguish and heartache over what he sees as Steve's betrayal of him. It is a graphic and literal depiction of Simon's sense of having been 'knifed through the heart'. Yet although this is a bleak card, it carries the promise that better times will eventually follow.

7 **Feelings** King of Swords

This is an uncompromising card, indicating someone who is hard and resolute. These can be useful attributes at times but they can also cut us off from the chance of reconciliation and compromise. Simon admitted that he was so angry with Steve that he did not know how he would ever bring himself to forgive him. The King of Swords can sometimes indicate someone who stops at nothing to impose their will, and Simon accepted that it might not be very helpful to deliberately set out to punish Steve even though he sometimes thought about it.

8 Outside influences King of Wands

In this position, the King of Wands refers to outside influences. It describes someone who is warm, supportive and positive, and Simon decided that it referred to his brother, Charles. Wands rule travel, and Charles had been suggesting that they went on holiday together so Simon could have a rest from the situation and then return to it refreshed. This seemed like a good idea and Simon said he was very tempted to do it.

9 Hopes and fears Eight of Wands

Here, the Eight of Wands describes Simon's hopes and fears. It seems that he is worried about taking hasty decisions without thinking the situation through properly. This card is especially associated with travel, and when asked whether this held any fears for him he said he was worried that he would return from his holiday with his brother to discover that Steve had moved out without telling him.

10 The outcome/resolution Two of Wands

This is a hopeful card when describing the resolution of the situation because it shows that Simon will soon be able to take stock of where he stands. Once again, travel is accentuated by this card, reiterating the tarot's earlier suggestion that Simon was in need of a holiday. As we talked, he accepted that he would be unable to stop Steve moving out and said he felt more resigned to the possibility of the relationship breaking up, if that turned out to be inevitable.

the horoscope spread

This is a classic spread for looking at every area of your life. It uses the astrological concept that the horoscope is divided into twelve sections, or houses, that govern these different areas. Usually, the Horoscope Spread shows what is happening in each area of your life, but here it has been adapted to look at the relationships that are associated with each astrological house.

Note the difference between the relationships described in the fifth, seventh and eighth houses. The fifth house encompasses love affairs, as well as relationships with your children and also with your favourite people. Seventh-house relationships describe committed one-to-one partnerships, such as marriage. They can also describe open enemies, as opposed to the hidden enemies denoted by the twelfth house. Eighth-house relationships share something, such as sex or money. So, if you are married, you would interpret the seventh house as being your relationship with your partner and the eighth house as what you share with them.

Sophie was feeling out of sorts after moving to a new area where she did not feel as settled as she had hoped. This reading took place at a time when she was feeling particularly vulnerable. Her new home was full of builders, her new neighbours were annoyed with her because of the renovations and she was going through a very busy time at work. While Sophie was shuffling the cards, the Emperor fell out of the deck and landed on the floor. Sophie took this to mean that she had more control over her relationships than she had realised and that sometimes she needed to assert more authority over people.

When analysed, this spread contained one Wands card, two Swords cards, three Pentacles cards and four Cups cards. There were only two Major Arcana cards, meaning Sophie has substantial control over her relationships and there were three court cards, indicating the important role that other people are playing in her life at the moment.

older friends and relatives,
authority figures

friends,
groups

teachers,
mentors

secret relationships,
hidden enemies

intimate partners,
financial partners

your relationship
with yourself

one-to-one relationships,
open enemies

what you value in
relationships

colleagues, customers,
employees

neighbours,
close relatives

children, love affairs,
favourite people

family members

11
Sophie's friends
Eight of Cups

QUEEN of CUPS

10
Sophie's older
friends and relativ
Queen of Cups

12
Sophie's hidden
relationships
Four of Swords

1
Sophie's relationship
with herself
Four of Cups

THE LOVERS

2
what Sophie values
in relationships
The Lovers

3
Sophie's neighbours
and close relatives
Seven of Cups

PAGE of SWORDS

4
Sophie's family
relationships
Page of Swords

186

9
**Sophie's teachers
and mentors**

Nine of Swords

8
**Sophie's intimate
relationships**

Page of Cups

7
**Sophie's one-to-one
relationships**

Eight of Wands

6
**Sophie's working
relationships**

Death

5
**Sophie's favourite
relationships**

Seven of Pentacles

187

1 Sophie's relationship with herself
Four of Cups

Sophie is comfortable with herself at the moment and in a more stable position than she imagines. Yet this card indicates that she is reluctant to take personal risks because she is worried about what she will lose as a result. She admitted that she felt her emotional expenditure was already pretty high and she sometimes wondered how much more she had to give.

2 What Sophie values in relationships
The Lovers

She needs a great deal of intimacy and a sense that she is united with others. The Lovers is ruled by Gemini, which is the sign that always searches for its twin. This shows that Sophie is always looking for kindred spirits with whom she can feel tremendous empathy and she really values this when she experiences it with others.

3 Sophie's neighbours and close relatives
Seven of Cups

In all the relationships Sophie currently has with neighbours and close relatives, one will be much more rewarding and exciting than she imagines. She must guard against taking people at face value because she is not reading them as well as she thinks. People who appear to be pleasant may turn out to be less so, while the reverse may also apply.

4 Sophie's family relationships Page of Swords

Sophie needs to use her insight when handling a particular member of her family. This person, who is young but not necessarily a man, may not be entirely honest or might accidentally send out mixed messages. Sophie thought that it might refer to her younger sister. Even if this person does not set out intentionally to deceive they may still create a lot of confusion. Perhaps Sophie should be wary of taking sides if a family dispute arises.

5 Sophie's favourite relationships
Seven of Pentacles

This is a good card when referring to love affairs and favourite relationships because it shows that Sophie can draw on the affection of others. There is no need for her to feel lonely or unloved because many people hold her in high esteem. It also indicates that the more love she shows others, the more she will receive in return. She will reap what she sows.

6 Sophie's working relationships Death
This is a card of endings, and Sophie laughingly suggested it meant the builders would soon be moving out of her house. It might well indicate this but it could have a deeper meaning because it is a Major Arcana card, suggesting that at least one of Sophie's working relationships will undergo a major change. She might sever a connection or alter it in some way, perhaps by changing jobs and finding something more fulfilling. But she would miss her colleagues.

7 Sophie's one-to-one relationships
Eight of Wands

Sophie is married, so this card represents some aspects of her relationship with her husband and it warns against rushing into any hasty decisions that they may later regret. The card has links with travel, so perhaps Sophie and her husband would benefit from having a restful holiday. It also describes the busy time the couple have had since their last house move.

8 Sophie's intimate relationships
Page of Cups

Life will improve for Sophie and her husband. In fact, it suggests that things will soon start to blossom for them, bringing them happiness and contentment. They will enjoy sharing creative or spiritual experiences. One way to do this may be in taking the time to decorate their new house so it becomes the restful haven they both crave.

9   Sophie's teachers and mentors
Nine of Swords

There are two so-called negative cards in this reading, and here is one of them. It indicates worry about someone who Sophie regards as a mentor or teacher. She agreed that she was concerned about a friend with whom she shared a spiritual philosophy and who was currently experiencing a very difficult time. However, this card suggests that she may be worrying unduly and things are perhaps not as bad as they seem.

10 Sophie's older friends and relatives
Queen of Cups

Here is a woman who can give Sophie a great deal of affection and support in her work. She will encourage Sophie to express herself confidently. Yet the card also indicates that Sophie should have more faith in her own abilities and talents, especially when it comes to trusting her intuition, creativity and imagination. This echoes the message of the Emperor, which fell out of the deck while Sophie was shuffling it.

11 Sophie's friends   Eight of Cups

This is the other difficult card. It suggests that a friendship or group connection will come to an end and Sophie will walk away from a relationship or situation, accepting that nothing more can be gained from it. This will be poignant but inevitable. Sophie thought this confirmed that she would change jobs and therefore say goodbye to her current colleagues

12 Sophie's hidden relationships
Four of Swords

This card suggests that recent problems with neighbours will come to an end. The tarot is making a joke here because it indicates that everyone concerned will hang up their swords. This will allow Sophie to relax and to put the entire experience behind her.

personal history spread

There are times when it is very helpful to gain an overview of what has been happening in a relationship during the past few months or years. What has really been going on and what has your general state of mind been? What has the other person been experiencing? How have your attitudes changed during the course of the relationship? Are you growing further apart or closer together, or are you stuck in a rut?

This spread will enable you to see what has been taking place during the past two years, months, weeks or days. If you are in a long-term relationship, you might like to examine what has been happening during the past two years. Alternatively, if things have been very eventful between you recently or you have only just met, you may prefer to look at the past two months or even weeks. If the situation is changing almost by the hour, it would probably be most helpful to examine the past two days. There are no rules about this and you can use more cards to look further back in time. However, before you begin the reading you must decide which timescale you will be using to avoid any confusion.

This spread does not show an outcome to the situation. Instead, it looks at what has contributed to it over a specific period of time. Other spreads, such as the Horoscope or Pyramid, can be used to examine the possible outcome.

1 your attitude two years/months ago

2 their attitude two years/months ago

5 your attitude now

3 your attitude one year/month ago

6 their attitude now

4 their attitude one year/month ago

1
Angie's
attitude
two years
ago

The Lovers

2
Jim's
attitude
two years
ago

Ten of
Pentacles

5
Angie's
attitude now

Ace of Wands

6
Jim's
attitude
now

Two of
Pentacle

3
Angie's
attitude
one year
ago

Ten of
Wands

4
Jim's attitude
one year ago

The Moon

Jim and Angie have been married for ten years. When they
first met they both felt that they had found their soulmate, and
they became inseparable almost immediately. However, what
was originally a fairytale relationship had become more
difficult over the years, not helped by an affair that Angie had
two years earlier. By the time Angie requested a reading they
were seriously considering splitting up.

The reading was given in April 2002 and the timescale
chosen was years. Therefore the cards in positions one
and two refer to what had happened in 2000, with the cards
in positions three and four detailing the events in 2001, and
cards five and six describing the situation at the time of the
reading in 2002.

There are two Major Arcana cards, which is an average number for a spread of this size. There are two Wands, two Pentacles and two Tens. It is the Tens that are most interesting, since it is unusual to find two of them in a spread of only six cards. Ten is the number of culmination, showing that both Jim and Angie have reached a turning point.

1   Angie's attitude two years ago   The Lovers

This card sometimes describes an eternal triangle and Angie admitted that she started an extra-marital affair in January 2000. It continued for the rest of the year and meant that she was completely torn between Jim and her lover. In the end, when her lover forced her to make a choice, she opted to stay with Jim. At the time, she promised herself that she would never tell Jim about the affair, and she never has.

2   Jim's attitude two years ago   Ten of Pentacles

Life was sweet for Jim in 2000. He was doing very well at work and earning a lot of money, which he enjoyed spending. Although this card indicates happiness and material benefits, it also warns against complacency and a tendency to take others for granted. Angie admitted that Jim seemed determined to ignore the cracks that were developing in their relationship.

3   Angie's attitude one year ago   Ten of Wands

In 2001, Angie took refuge in work. She was still smarting from the break-up of her affair and needed to distract herself. Her job in advertising had always been exciting and stimulating, but after her office was restructured her job began to feel like an unsustainable burden. She said she 'plodded along' both at home and at work, yet felt unable to raise the problem of her failing marriage with Jim. Everything seemed to be beyond her.

4   Jim's attitude one year ago   The Moon

After the heady days of 2000, 2001 was characterised by confusion and doubt for Jim, as shown by the Moon. He became depressed and started drinking heavily. This card can describe deception, and Jim convinced himself that Angie was having an affair. Angie found this deeply ironic because Jim had remained blissfully ignorant when she really was having an affair. Eventually, Jim decided to see a counsellor because he felt unable to cope any longer.

5 Angie's attitude now Ace of Wands

This is a much more positive card for Angie, and it suggests that she will soon become involved in an exciting venture that might include travel. Indeed, a few days before the reading took place she had applied for a new job that would entail several long journeys each year. She is optimistic about the future of her career but is still undecided about whether to continue with her marriage.

6 Jim's attitude now Two of Pentacles

Life is still a struggle for Jim and he is busily trying to juggle the demands of his job with the need to shore up his marriage. Angie feels that he is only just managing to keep his head above water, which is an apt metaphor because this card often shows a rolling sea in the background. She has decided that she should be of more help to him in the future, particularly by giving him increased emotional support.

When events are moving very fast, you can use the Personal History Spread to examine what has been happening during the past few months, weeks or even days. This second reading explores the developments that took place between Derek and Paula, who first met two months before they came for a reading. At the time, Derek, an accountant, was out of work and decided to sign up with an employment agency. Paula, who owned the agency, interviewed him. Having recently been divorced after a very turbulent marriage, she tried to resist her attraction to Derek because she did not want to risk any more heartbreak. However, Derek won her over and, at the time of the reading, the couple were thinking of getting married. The timescale chosen here is months.

1
Derek's attitude two months ago

Six of Pentacles

2
Paula's attitude two months ago

Two of Wands

5
Derek's attitude now

The World

6
Paula's attitude now

The Lovers

3
Derek's attitude one month ago

Two of Cups

4
Paula's attitude one month ago

The Hermit

1 Derek's attitude two months ago Six of Pentacles

Sometimes the tarot describes situations in very accurate detail, and here is an example of this. The Six of Pentacles can show someone in need of money, as was Derek when he first met Paula at the agency. The Pentacles suit reflects his work as an accountant. There is nothing romantic about this card, and when Derek first met Paula his mind was not on relationships.

2 Paula's attitude two months ago Two of Wands

One of the meanings of this card is that an opportunity is on the way, although the person concerned does not yet know it.

For Paula, the opportunity was the chance to meet Derek and fall in love with him. The Two of Wands describes someone who has a good vantage point and who is doing well, as was Paula two months ago when she first met Derek.

3 Derek's attitude one month ago Two of Cups

One month ago, Derek was certain that he loved Paula and was hoping that his feelings were reciprocated. The Two of Cups is a classic indication of a long-term relationship and possibly even marriage, which was certainly on Derek's mind by this time. They were dating, but Derek was taking things slowly because he did not want to frighten Paula.

4 Paula's attitude one month ago The Hermit

Paula was very torn and did not know what to do. She suspected she was falling in love with Derek, and the knowledge scared her because she did not think she was ready for another long-term relationship. She tried to play for time. This card shows her caution and emotional retreat from the situation. She also confided in a friend whose opinion she respects.

5 Derek's attitude now The World

Derek is willing to risk everything in order to be with Paula. The World is a card of culmination, and Derek certainly feels that he has finally found someone he can spend the rest of his life with. He says that walking into Paula's employment agency was the best decision he ever made.

6 Paula's attitude now The Lovers

As this card shows, Paula is now ready to give love a chance. Nevertheless, the Lovers can sometimes indicate that a choice must be made, and perhaps a part of Paula is still unsure whether to commit herself to Derek and risk having her heart broken. Although it is too early to tell how the relationship will work out, this card suggests that Derek and Paula will be very happy together.

healing relationship spread

This is an ideal spread to use when you want to examine a relationship and discover what to do about it. It is especially useful if your relationship is essentially sound but needs a little work, particularly if you have been together a long time and have a tendency to take each other for granted. It allows you to study what is preventing you from finding a resolution to your difficulties and also to see how you can move these forward. In addition, it shows you what you both need, which may be at the heart of the dilemma. The final card describes the outcome.

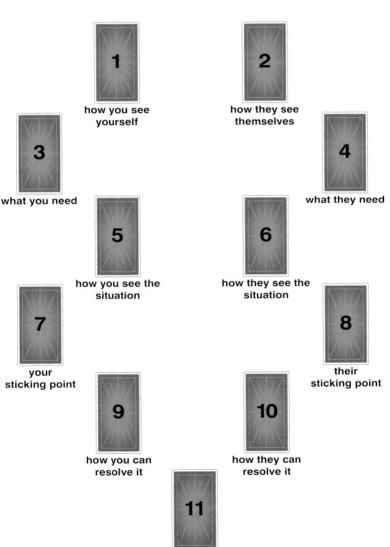

1 how you see yourself

2 how they see themselves

3 what you need

4 what they need

5 how you see the situation

6 how they see the situation

7 your sticking point

8 their sticking point

9 how you can resolve it

10 how they can resolve it

11 the outcome

1
**how Anna
sees herself**

Seven of Wands

2
**how Greg
sees himself**

Queen of Pentacle[s]

3
**what Anna
needs**

Six of Wands

4
**what Greg
needs**

King of Wands

5
**how Anna sees
the situation**

Two of Wands

6
**how Greg sees the
situation**

Queen of Wands

7
**Anna's sticking
point**

Four of Pentacles

8
**Greg's sticking
point**

The Star

9
**how Anna can
resolve it**

King of Swords

10
**how Greg can
resolve it**

Page of Cups

11
the outcome

Five of
Pentacles

Anna and Greg have lived together for five years but have now reached a crisis in their relationship. Greg is happy for things to continue as they are; Anna wants to get married and have a family. She feels that her biological clock is ticking and that she will miss the chance to have children if Greg does not make this commitment. Greg has a very demanding and well-paid career as a barrister, and says he has little spare time to devote to children. He also says he is happy with the way things are. Anna is thinking of giving him an ultimatum.

There are three striking factors about this reading. First, there is only one card from the Major Arcana, indicating that Anna and Greg can resolve the problem if they are prepared to work at it. Second, there are five Wands cards, which rule negotiations, travel and the clever use of words, suggesting that they need to talk things through and find compromises. Third, there are five court cards, four of which describe Greg's side of the story. This implies that other people are involved in the situation, perhaps offering advice or hoping for a particular outcome that will benefit them.

Anna requested the reading after a particularly turbulent weekend during which she and Greg had argued almost non-stop about whether to get married.

1 **How Anna sees herself** Seven of Wands

This card describes having to fend off competition and rivalry. When this was mentioned to Anna, she admitted that she felt jealous of one of Greg's female colleagues, whom she finds very predatory. She knows they are friends but suspects that the woman wants something more and is subtly trying to undermine Anna in Greg's eyes.

2 **How Greg sees himself** Queen of Pentacles

Although this card depicts a woman, it describes Greg's busy career and the money it brings him. It shows that he feels he is already providing a stable and comfortable environment for Anna. There is also a suggestion of Greg's female colleague here, indicating that she is talking to him about the situation and that she may be trying to influence his decision.

3 What Anna needs Six of Wands

The Six of Wands here suggests that Anna needs plenty of
appreciation and moral support, especially in her career. When
this was mentioned to her, she said she felt her career had to
take second place to Greg's and that it was not accorded
enough importance in their relationship. When they discuss
their jobs, Greg's work usually gets the most attention.

4 What Greg needs King of Wands

This card describes a generous, warm-hearted man who is full
of enthusiasm and ideas. He takes things lightly and is good
fun. Anna said this was a side of Greg that she had not seen so
often recently and which she therefore suspected was being
suppressed for some reason. She thought it may be because
their conversations revolved around marriage and often led to
disputes. The fun was going out of their relationship.

5 How Anna sees the situation Two of Wands

The Two of Wands describes the ability to take an overview
of a situation and to gain some perspective. Anna is in a
good position to think things through and see what her next
step should be. However, she should guard against any
tendency to assume that she has the answers and that Greg
should go along with them regardless of his own feelings.

6 How Greg sees the situation Queen of Wands

Once again, a woman is representing Greg's viewpoint.
The Queen of Wands describes someone who prides
themselves on being able to combine their home life with
outside interests. This card also represents someone who
enjoys a busy social life and who does not take kindly to any
form of possessiveness. Perhaps Greg is feeling trapped by
Anna's demands?

7 Anna's sticking point Four of Pentacles

This card describes a reluctance to take risks, especially
financial ones, and a tendency to cling to the status quo
through fear of change. When we talked about this, Anna

agreed that she dreamt of a comfortable life in a large house with a husband and children, and was very threatened by the thought that she may not achieve this. She cannot envision any other future for herself.

8 Greg's sticking point The Star

This is one of the most favourable cards in the tarot because it represents wishes coming true and the end of difficult situations. It also describes the ability to combine spiritual and material pursuits, and suggests that Greg is more capable of this than Anna imagines. It offers a beacon of hope and shows that they can resolve their problems if they are both prepared to compromise.

9 How Anna can resolve it King of Swords

Anna must make some tough decisions based on reality rather than wishful thinking. The King of Swords is a very powerful figure and Anna needs to absorb some of his no-nonsense energy. This card can also suggest that it would be helpful to seek an expert opinion about something, which Anna has done by asking for a tarot reading.

10 How Greg can resolve it Page of Cups

Greg needs to take a more spiritual and holistic view of the situation. He must appreciate Anna's point of view while weighing up his own needs. This card describes someone who is compassionate, understanding and warm-hearted, which are some of the qualities that originally attracted Anna to Greg.

11 The outcome Five of Pentacles

The Five of Pentacles is sounding a strong warning that Anna and Greg are in danger of losing something very precious if they are not careful. They are so busy concentrating on their differences, and how miserable these make them, that they have forgotten how to enjoy each other's company. They must both think carefully about their priorities and find a way forward together.

the eternal triangle spread

Humans have doubtless been involved in eternal triangles since we first drew breath. Artists and writers have gained endless inspiration from them, sometimes presenting a rather romanticised view of these triangular relationships. Yet they are also the stuff of court cases involving divorces, murders and vendettas, and they can be anything but romantic for the protagonists. We may thrill to read about them in our morning newspapers but it is often a very different story if we become involved in an eternal triangle ourselves.

This spread is designed to look at a situation in which only three people are involved, such as a husband and wife, and her lover. If the lover also has a partner, you should use the Eternal Rectangle Spread which appears on page 208.

Before you lay out the cards for this spread it is essential that you decide which pile of cards will represent which person. Otherwise, you could become confused or be tempted to switch the positions once you see the cards, especially if you are one of the people involved in the triangle.

When Wendy came for a reading she was very distressed because her husband, Philip, had just found out about her love affair with one of their neighbours, who is a property developer. Things were at their worst between husband and wife, and they could barely speak to each other without having a row. Wendy's lover, Johnny, had broken off their affair because he was worried about losing his reputation, both socially and professionally. They all live in a small village and do not want their private drama to become the latest item of gossip.

One of the most striking elements of this reading is the number of court cards that appear. Yet this makes sense because it revolves largely around people and court cards reflect that. It is also notable that only one Major Arcana

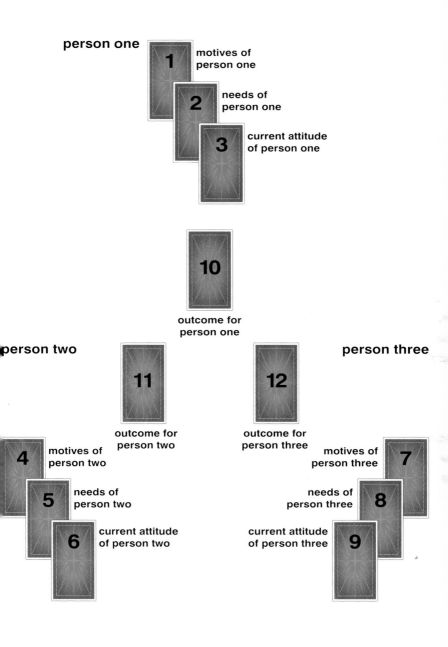

person one

1 — motives of person one

2 — needs of person one

3 — current attitude of person one

10 — outcome for person one

person two

person three

11 — outcome for person two

12 — outcome for person three

4 — motives of person two

5 — needs of person two

6 — current attitude of person two

7 — motives of person three

8 — needs of person three

9 — current attitude of person three

card appears, suggesting that the outcome of the situation rests almost entirely in the hands of the individuals involved. There are two Swords cards, four Wands, two Cups and three Pentacles, giving a good overall balance of the suits. There are also two Pages, two Sixes and two Eights.

1

Johnny's motives

Page of Pentacles

Johnny

2

Johnny's needs

Ace of Pentacles

3

Johnny's current attitude

Queen of Wands

10

the outcome for Johnny

Six of Swords

Wendy

4

Wendy's motives

Eight of Pentacles

5

Wendy's needs

Eight of Wands

6

Wendy's current attitude

Page of Swords

11

the outcome for Wendy

Ten of Wands

1 Johnny's motives Page of Pentacles

This card describes someone who is efficient and has a good head for business. As such, Johnny's motives involve his career and his earning power, suggesting that he did not intend to become involved in a potentially scandalous love affair with one of his neighbours. Pages represent situations that have only just begun, underlining Wendy's suspicion that Johnny was never as involved with her as she was with him.

2 Johnny's needs Ace of Pentacles

Here is another money card, suggesting that Johnny has a strong need to be seen as successful. Although the Ace of Pentacles can sometimes indicate an engagement or marriage, it seems that this was far from Johnny's mind. Instead, Wendy said that he was very materially minded and always looking for new ways to make money. It is interesting that they first got to know each other when Wendy gave him some specialist advice about one of his business ventures.

12

e outcome for Philip's

Six of Wands

Philip

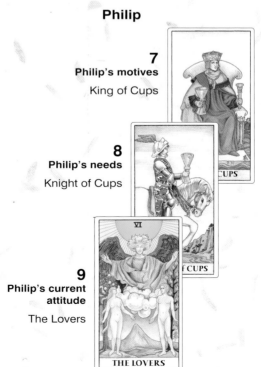

7

Philip's motives

King of Cups

8

Philip's needs

Knight of Cups

9

Philip's current attitude

The Lovers

3 Johnny's current attitude Queen of Wands

Anyone characterised by this card is able to juggle many demands on their time. They are capable of great warmth, but do not suffer fools gladly. This hints that Johnny is coping well with what has happened, perhaps because he cannot afford to behave differently. His reputation as a solid member of the community is obviously very important to him.

4 Wendy's motives Eight of Pentacles

Wendy was obviously looking for excitement and new challenges when she became involved with Johnny, because this card describes being able to make the most of one's gifts and abilities. She liked the way Johnny encouraged her to explore her talents and make the most of them. She said her marriage was going through an unexciting phase when she first became attracted to Johnny, and she instigated their relationship. He made her feel that she could do almost anything.

5 Wendy's needs Eight of Wands

Here is another indication that Wendy needed more excitement in her life when she first became involved with Johnny. This card suggests an enjoyably busy time in which things happen quickly. It is often associated with travel, and Wendy said that one of her dreams was to escape on a short foreign trip with Johnny. It never happened, much to her disappointment.

6 Wendy's current attitude Page of Swords

This is a slightly worrying card because it suggests that someone is not to be trusted. Wendy may have to fight against a tendency to drop hints to people about what has happened, and must take care not to let the cat out of the bag by accident.

7 Philip's motives King of Cups

Philip has always struggled to express his emotions. He gives the impression of being rather reserved, although he is capable of great passion and feeling. This card has spiritual connotations, and when Wendy's affair first began, Philip was rediscovering his religion, which he had neglected for years.

8 Philip's needs Knight of Cups

Here is another Cups court card, emphasising Philip's need for
love and emotional support. This Knight often describes a
spiritual or creative quest, which has recently become central to
Philip's life. It can also indicate that an opportunity will lead to
great changes and possibly even a new home, suggesting that
this difficult situation will ease for him and yield a silver lining.

9 Philip's current attitude The Lovers

Philip is clearly considering what to do and it will not be an
easy decision. There is often an element of sacrifice with this
card; Wendy admitted that Philip was unsure whether he could
cope with the upheaval of a separation, yet he found the
present circumstances intolerable. A separation and possible
divorce would also clash with his rediscovered faith.

10 The outcome for Johnny Six of Swords

The outcome for Johnny is that things will become easier in
time and he will feel calmer about the situation. This is not
an easy card so it hints that, despite appearances to the
contrary, Johnny is feeling beleaguered and worried about
what has happened. He may also be very wary about
getting involved in a similar situation in the future.

11 The outcome for Wendy Ten of Wands

For Wendy, life will feel like a struggle. However, it is likely that
things do not have to be as difficult as she will make them.
She may find more positive or constructive ways to approach
the situation, or she could decide to ask for help. This might
involve talking to a marriage guidance counsellor or even
talking to Philip, so they can work things through together.

12 The outcome for Philip Six of Wands

Of the three people involved, it looks as though Philip will have
the best outcome. This will require work but he will eventually
have good reason to feel proud of the way he has handled the
situation. He may become successful on a professional level
as well as in his marriage.

the eternal rectangle spread

Sometimes four people are involved in a tense relationship with one another. This might be because two couples are brought together through infidelity, with a partner from one couple having an affair with a partner from the other. Everyone is involved, even if they are simply on the sidelines. The Eternal Rectangle Spread will help you to see what is going on in this sort of complex relationship.

Rectangular relationships do not only arise out of infidelity, of course. They can operate in families, perhaps between parents and two of their children, or between four siblings. You might encounter them at work, with tensions between bosses and employees, or perhaps through rivalry between you and your colleagues.

The tarot is very useful when you want to unravel the dynamics of rectangular relationships. However, as always, you must make sure that you know exactly which pile of cards represents which person within the relationship. If necessary, write down each person's name on a slip of paper and place it in the relevant position so you can see quickly which cards refer to whom.

Sandra wanted a reading because she was experiencing problems with her parents, Barry and June, who are in their sixties. She was also struggling to get on with her maternal grandmother, Peggy, who is in her late eighties. Sandra is twenty-five and considers herself old enough to make her own decisions and mistakes; her parents and grandmother disagree. There are frequent arguments about Sandra's private life, and recently there was a massive disagreement when Sandra's latest boyfriend was deemed to be unacceptable and, to quote her mother, 'not good enough for her'. Although Sandra left home when she was twenty-one and moved to a neighbouring town, she still feels tied to her parents' apron strings and is becoming increasingly resentful about it. To make matters more complicated, Peggy has developed a serious heart problem and has moved in with June and Barry. June is insisting that Sandra does not do anything to

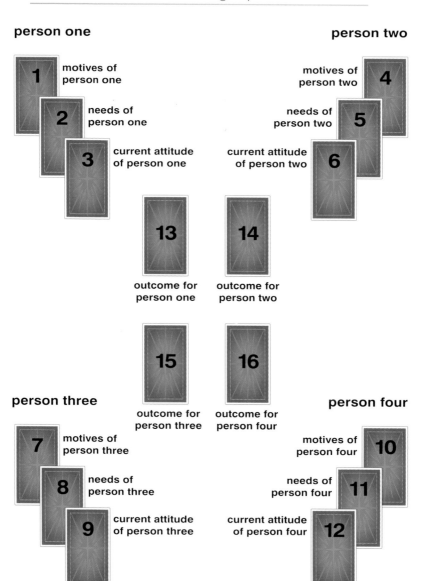

person one

1 motives of person one

2 needs of person one

3 current attitude of person one

person two

motives of person two 4

needs of person two 5

current attitude of person two 6

13 outcome for person one

14 outcome for person two

15 outcome for person three

16 outcome for person four

person three

7 motives of person three

8 needs of person three

9 current attitude of person three

person four

motives of person four 10

needs of person four 11

current attitude of person four 12

upset her grandmother during the remainder of her life. As far as Sandra is concerned, this is the final straw.

This spread contains sixteen cards so it is important to study them carefully before beginning the reading because there may well be a high proportion of cards from a particular suit, number or Arcana. Here, there are six cards from the Major Arcana, which is not very notable. Nevertheless, two of them refer to Sandra's position and two to Barry's, which suggests that they both have a lot to learn from the situation.

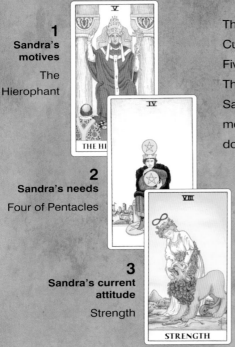

1
Sandra's motives
The Hierophant

2
Sandra's needs
Four of Pentacles

3
Sandra's current attitude
Strength

There are four Pentacles, three Cups, one Wand, two Swords, two Fives, two Fours and three Threes. The four Pentacles are telling Sandra to deal with the present moment, and to be practical when doing so. The Threes indicate that

Sandra

June

13
the outcome for Sandra
Queen of Pentacles

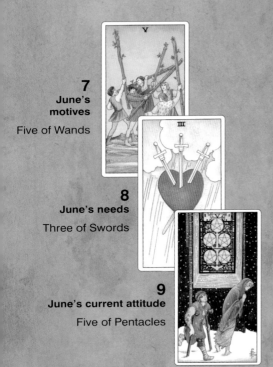

7
June's motives
Five of Wands

8
June's needs
Three of Swords

9
June's current attitude
Five of Pentacles

15
the outcome for June
The Empress

the situation is in a process of
change. While Sandra was
shuffling the cards, the Six of
Swords fell out, suggesting that
the problem will eventually resolve
itself but it will cause much guilt
and worry in the meantime.

4
Barry's motives
Three of
Pentacles

5
Barry's needs
The Sun

6
**Barry's current
attitude**
The World

14
the outcome for Barry
Four of Cups

Barry

Peggy

16
the outcome for Peggy
King of Cups

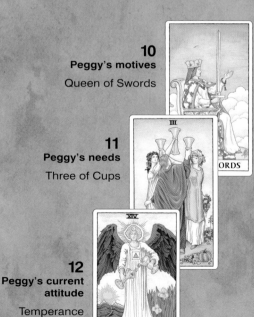

10
Peggy's motives
Queen of Swords

11
Peggy's needs
Three of Cups

12
**Peggy's current
attitude**
Temperance

1 Sandra's motives The Hierophant

This card shows that Sandra does not deliberately want to stir up dissent among her family and that she is actually more conventional than they imagine. She wants to behave in ways that she can live with, and which she feels will not clash with her spiritual beliefs. At the time of the reading she was considering talking about the situation to a friend whom she considers to be a mentor.

2 Sandra's needs Four of Pentacles

Sandra has a strong need to maintain the status quo and not to do things that will upset other people. This card describes a reluctance to step out of one's comfort zone into areas that do not feel as safe or familiar, especially if these will have an adverse effect financially. Sandra said she felt unable to break her connection with her family even though she was sometimes tempted to do so. She admitted that her parents often gave her money to help her through lean patches and she would struggle to manage without their assistance.

3 Sandra's current attitude Strength

When she came for the reading, Sandra seemed quite stoical and matter-of-fact, as shown by this card. She was cheered when told that Strength indicates an ability to weather storms and to cope with difficult situations. She felt it was important to reach an understanding with her parents, yet wanted to stand her ground over issues when necessary. She decided that it might be helpful to be less financially reliant on her parents in the future.

4 Barry's motives Three of Pentacles

It is clear from this card that Barry only wants the best for his daughter. He considers all the time and effort that he has spent on her upbringing are an investment for her future. Classic illustrations of this card often show an architect discussing his plans with his clients, which made Sandra laugh because her father is an architect. She suggested that perhaps he viewed her as his greatest project.

5 Barry's needs The Sun

The Sun often refers to children, and here it describes Barry's need for his daughter's love and attention. Sandra said that her father seemed much more tolerant of her choices than her mother and grandmother, and that he sometimes defended her in arguments. She found this card heartening because it suggested that her father was much more supportive of her than she sometimes imagined and that, above all, he loved her.

6 Barry's current attitude The World

The World often describes the end of one cycle and the beginning of another. Sandra said that Barry's attitude to the situation had recently begun to change and that he was becoming more supportive of her. He was taking her side against her mother more often, for which she was grateful. When tactfully asked whether she considered that her father was henpecked, she readily agreed and said that he had recently started to be more assertive. 'The worm is turning,' she laughed.

7 June's motives Five of Wands

This is the first of three difficult cards for June. It shows that her motives in the situation are to assert herself against what she considers to be difficult circumstances. Life is a struggle for her. Sandra said that June had always been bossed about by her own mother, Peggy, and that when she was growing up she was very conscious of being plain, while her two younger sisters were very pretty. Sandra said that sometimes her mother had hinted at a sense of rivalry between them for Barry's affection.

8 June's needs Three of Swords

Sandra gasped when she saw this card because it reminded her of June's habit of clutching her heart during family rows (the illustration shows a heart pierced with three swords). As such, it is also a powerful reminder of Peggy's heart problems, about which June is worried. It shows that June feels she has been emotionally wounded and needs comfort. It may also suggest that sometimes June plays on her sense of being wounded and betrayed.

9 June's current attitude Five of Pentacles

This card indicates that June feels impoverished and alone. She is frightened of losing something precious, yet this is exactly what will happen if she continues with her current behaviour. Sandra began to feel more compassionate towards her mother when she realised how much she had been suffering. Although June may be unable to do much about her mother's illness, she might be able to repair her relationship with her daughter in time.

10 Peggy's motives Queen of Swords

The Queen of Swords describes a woman who has learned to survive by being emotionally resilient and possibly rather tough. Sandra said this summed up Peggy perfectly, because she is a martinet. She sees herself as the head of the family and likes to believe that her word is law. According to Sandra, Peggy had done her best to live June's life for her because she did not want her to make the same mistakes that Peggy believed she had made.

11 Peggy's needs Three of Cups

In striking contrast to the stern authority of the Queen of Swords, this shows that Peggy needs to be surrounded by the warmth of female company and the conviviality of a close-knit group of people. Sandra laughed out loud at this, saying that Peggy had a strange way of showing it. Nevertheless, she admitted that there was a much softer side to Peggy and that she could be very affectionate at times.

12 Peggy's current attitude Temperance

This is an interesting card because it suggests that Peggy is currently reviewing her life and some of the actions she has taken. In view of her serious health problems and her advanced age, perhaps Peggy is preparing herself for death. Sandra said that Peggy had seemed more reflective recently and was also less convinced that she was always in the right.

13 The outcome for Sandra Queen of Pentacles

When looking at the outcome for Sandra, this card neatly follows on from what was discussed when looking at the Four of Pentacles. It shows a woman who is in control of her money and who has a successful job. It inspired Sandra to take more responsibility for the state of her finances and to actively start looking for a better-paid job that would give her more financial independence from her parents.

14 The outcome for Barry Four of Cups

Barry will soon be offered an interesting opportunity but the question is whether he will be aware of it. He may not want to be bothered with it, or it may present too much of a challenge. It is possible that the opportunity is the chance he needs to alter his relationship with the rest of the family and to break some of the habits he has fallen into with them. Sandra said she would do her best to encourage him in this.

15 The outcome for June The Empress

This is a very favourable card for June, because it suggests that she will develop the softer side of her personality and will become more openly affectionate. The Empress denotes fertility and abundance, and sometimes describes a house move. Although June had no plans to move house at the time of the reading, Sandra wondered whether her parents would move after Peggy died and if it would be a liberation for June.

16 The outcome for Peggy King of Cups

Peggy needs to be encouraged to be more loving and affectionate. As a result, she may realise that she can maintain the position of authority she craves without having to behave like a harridan and make everyone's lives a misery. She may also gain greater peace of mind, despite the health difficulties that are facing her.

heart of the matter spread

This is an in-depth spread that allows you to study various aspects of your life in detail. It provides plenty of food for thought but is quite complicated, so is not really suitable if you have only just learned how to read the tarot. Nevertheless, once you are more familiar with it you can begin to enjoy using this spread.

This reading differs from the others in the book because you have to group together the cards that refer to particular situations. For instance, you must read the two obstacle cards together, and also read the four current influence cards together. For this reason, the reading does not run in chronological order. It shows what is going on but does not offer solutions. However, you can discover these using other spreads if necessary.

This was a reading for Pierre, who felt he was stuck in a rut. This sense of being stuck extended to his relationship with his wife, Monique, and also to his job as an estate agent. What he really wanted was to change careers and train to become a vet. However, his wife was worried about how this would affect their income and was very resistant to the idea.

In this reading there were only three Major Arcana cards, indicating that Pierre had greater control over the situation than he imagined. There were three Swords, three Pentacles, three Wands and one Cups card, so no suit was predominant. The two Aces show the need for a fresh start.

1 Current influence Nine of Swords

This card denotes worry, although there are hints that it is disproportionate to the problem and things are not really as bad as they seem. Very often, this worry is so strong that it can keep someone awake at night. Pierre admitted that he had been having sleepless nights because he had been unsure what to do for the best.

5 Current influence The Hanged Man

Here, Pierre feels in limbo, unable to make any progress at the moment. It perfectly describes his sensation of 'being

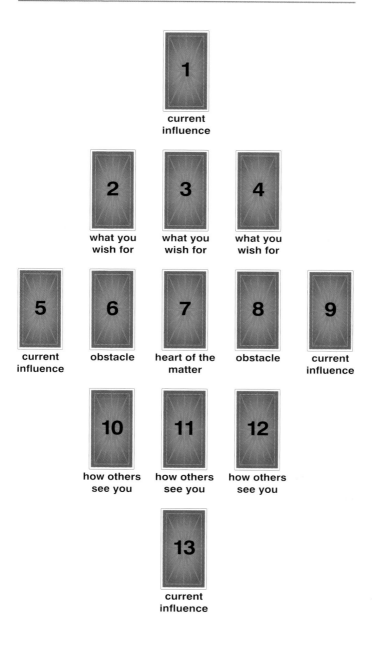

1
current
influence

2
what you
wish for

3
what you
wish for

4
what you
wish for

5
current
influence

6
obstacle

7
heart of the
matter

8
obstacle

9
current
influence

10
how others
see you

11
how others
see you

12
how others
see you

13
current
influence

between the devil and the deep blue sea', as he put it. He did not want to continue to be an estate agent but was worried about putting additional stress on his marriage by retraining to be a vet. The Hanged Man can encourage us to look at situations from a different point of view, so it suggests that perhaps Pierre should try to understand his wife's anxieties.

1
current influence
Nine of Swords

2
what Pierre wishes for
Ace of Pentacles

3
what Pierre wishes fo
The Sun

5
current influence
The Hanged Man

6
obstacle
Two of Swords

7
heart of the matter
Ace of Wands

10
how others see Pierre
Knight of Pentacles

11
how others see Pierre
Queen of Wands

13
current influence
Two of Pentacles

9 Current influence Seven of Cups

In normal circumstances this is an encouraging card because it suggests that an exciting opportunity will soon present itself. The trick will be in recognising it when it does appear and not being seduced by the empty promises of other opportunities that will also materialise. This simply confused Pierre and increased his frustration of not knowing whether he should make the best of his current circumstances or try something new.

4
at Pierre wishes for
Seven of Swords

8
obstacle
The Fool

9
current influence
Seven of Cups

12
w others see Pierre
Ten of Wands

13 Current influence
Two of Pentacles

Pierre laughed when he saw this card because he said it was an apt description of how he felt in having to juggle his own needs and those of Monique. He could not see any way of finding a compromise between his need to do something different with his life and her reluctance to scale down her living standards. Very often this card describes a choice that will involve some form of financial sacrifice, as does the Hanged Man (page 46).

2 What Pierre wishes for Ace of Pentacles

This card shows Pierre's need for new beginnings and challenges. One of its traditional meanings is a change of career or direction, so it vividly describes what Pierre is wishing for. It also shows his need to make money from his new venture.

3 What Pierre wishes for The Sun

This is one of the most creative cards in the entire deck, again showing Pierre's need to spread his wings and express himself in new ways. It is very hard to blot out the light of the sun, so the presence of this card in this position suggests it will be very difficult for Pierre to subdue his yearning to retrain as a vet.

4 What Pierre wishes for Seven of Swords

Perhaps not surprisingly, it seems that Pierre would like to steal away from his current difficulties. He would be happy to concede on some points if he could come away feeling that he had gained more than he had lost. There is a sneaky atmosphere to this card and a sense that someone may not be playing fair. Pierre admitted that he had wondered whether to solve the problem by presenting Monique with a fait accompli and seeing what happened next.

6 Obstacle Two of Swords

Money is the main obstacle for Pierre and here is one of the classic cards describing money trouble. Yet it also talks about the fear of seeing a situation in its true light, suggesting that Pierre and Monique are allowing their fears of financial loss to dominate every other consideration. It is therefore urging Pierre to examine his options in more detail before making a decision.

8 Obstacle The Fool

This is one of the cards of bold, new beginnings. Yet the Fool always raises questions about these fresh starts, asking whether they are foolhardy or whether other people's objections to them are unfounded. When representing an obstacle, as it does here, it clearly describes Monique's misgivings about Pierre's planned change of career.

7 **Heart of the Matter** Ace of Wands

At the heart of the matter is Pierre's need to begin afresh. Wands rule enterprise, risks and career aspirations, so this card is clearly stating Pierre's dilemma. Should he risk everything by trying something new or play safe and possibly always regret it? The card is so encouraging, and so relevant to his situation, that it is tempting to believe it is urging him to go ahead with his plans.

10 **How others see Pierre** Knight of Pentacles

This is the first of the three cards that describe how others see Pierre, and is very interesting because the Knight of Pentacles refers to someone who is seen to be very solid, reliable and trustworthy. This is not someone who takes risks, especially with money. It therefore suggests that when Monique first met Pierre she saw him as someone who would never compromise her happiness or living standards.

11 **How others see Pierre** Queen of Wands

The Queen of Wands describes someone who is successful in business and who is able to combine their domestic life with their career. They have a natural authority but also a tremendous warmth. Pierre said that this described Monique perfectly, so the fact that the card describes how *she* sees him suggests that she may be projecting a lot of her own needs on to him. Perhaps she would also like to take more risks than she allows herself to do?

12 **How others see Pierre** Ten of Wands

Someone in Pierre's life thinks he is struggling with a heavy burden but that he could reduce it and the sheer confusion that it is causing may be preventing him from seeing the way forward. Pierre said that his best friend kept telling him not to make a meal out of the situation and simply to get on with it; he admitted that he had a tendency to make mountains out of molehills and also to be defeated by problems when they became too great.

the karma spread

Why do certain people come into our lives? Most of us have had relationships that feel very significant, whether for good or ill. Some people are convinced that they have known someone in a previous life because they seem so familiar or they share such strong emotional links. We might be absolutely certain that we have met someone for a particular reason, usually because we love them and they bring us joy. Yet we can learn a lot from our more difficult relationships, too, especially if we are prepared to examine our motives with some degree of objectivity.

This is called the Karma Spread because it enables you to explore a relationship in detail, both from your own perspective and from that of the other person. You can use it for any sort of relationship, although you may find it most informative when examining one that is stressful because it will give you greater understanding of what is going on between all those involved.

Richard came for a reading because he was struggling to have a civil relationship with his stepfather, Tony. Tony had been married to Richard's mother, Elaine, for three years, during which time the atmosphere between stepfather and stepson had deteriorated drastically. Although Richard, who is in his early twenties, no longer lives at home he still likes to visit Elaine, but has recently started to dream up excuses for not going as frequently as he once did. He says Tony is rude to him, which he suspects is caused by jealousy, and that he is always finding fault with him. Tony likes to deliberate over decisions, and is rather stuck in his ways. Richard's younger brother, Paul, still lives at home and gets on quite well with Tony.

What is most noticeable about this spread is the four court cards, indicating that several people are involved in the situation and also that some people may be interfering or meddling. There are three Major Arcana cards, which is the average number for this size of spread. There are four Cups, two Pentacles and three Swords, so the emphasis on Cups suggests that Richard is emotionally involved in the situation and may not be as objective as he imagines. As the cards describe, it seems that Richard and Tony have a lot to learn from each other.

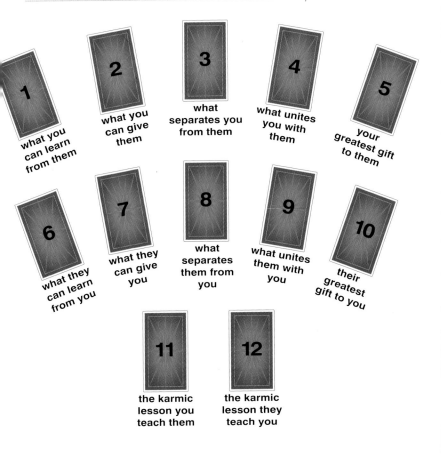

1 through 10 card layout with the following position labels:

1 — what you can learn from them
2 — what you can give them
3 — what separates you from them
4 — what unites you with them
5 — your greatest gift to them
6 — what they can learn from you
7 — what they can give you
8 — what separates them from you
9 — what unites them with you
10 — their greatest gift to you
11 — the karmic lesson you teach them
12 — the karmic lesson they teach you

1 What Richard can learn from Tony Judgement

This is the card of the second chance, implying that the
relationship may improve in time. It suggests that Richard
should try to give Tony another chance and not to judge him
too harshly, even though this may be difficult. Perhaps there
are mitigating factors of which Richard is not aware, or
maybe he is being overly critical of Tony and only
concentrating on what he sees as his bad points.

2 What Richard can give Tony Knight of Swords

This is a card of action and rapid decision-making, so perhaps
Richard could help Tony to liven up a little or at least to
become less stuck in a rut. Richard was not sure how he
could do this, given Tony's resistance to him. Nevertheless, an
occasion might arise in the future, so Richard should take note
of the meaning of this card in case it comes in handy later on.

1
what Richard can
learn from Tony
Judgement

2
what Richard can
give Tony
Knight of Swords

6
what Tony can
learn from Richard
The Sun

7
what Tony can
give Richard
Nine of Swords

11
the karmic lesson
Richard teaches Tony
Two of Cups

3 What separates Richard from Tony Six of Cups

The Six of Cups represents nostalgia, and is a vivid description of what separates the two men. Richard cannot help remembering how things used to be so much happier when his father was alive, and therefore unfavourably compares the present with his rosy view of the past. If Richard continues to look back over his shoulder to happier times, he will never be able to resolve his differences with Tony.

3
what separates
Richard from Tony
Six of Cups

4
what unites
Richard with Tony
Ten of Cups

5
Richard's greatest
gift to Tony
Queen of Pentacles

8
what separates
Tony from Richard
Queen of Swords

9
what unites
Tony with Richard
Page of Pentacles

10
Tony's greatest
gift to Richard
The Star

12
the karmic lesson
Tony teaches Richard
Five of Cups

4 What unites Richard with Tony Ten of Cups

This is very encouraging because it represents the pinnacle
of joy, happiness and a contented home life. It seems that
both Richard and Tony want the same thing. When we talked
about this, we agreed that Richard had to play his part in
creating a more comfortable atmosphere by being more
accepting of Tony, and understanding that Tony sometimes
felt envious of Richard's relationship with his dead father.

5 Richard's greatest gift to Tony
Queen of Pentacles

Richard thought this card referred to his mother, Elaine, who fits the description of the Queen of Pentacles: a woman who combines a heavy workload with running a family. He felt it was telling him that his greatest gift to Tony was not to stand in the way of his marriage to Elaine, and to accept that there must be good reasons why Elaine chose to marry him.

6 What Tony can learn from Richard The Sun

Tony can learn a lot about happiness, creativity and spontaneity from Richard as well as how to be more affectionate and warm. In begining to meet some of Richard's needs, he may also be able to meet some of his own in the process. This card can refer to becoming a parent, so perhaps Tony will learn how to become a true parent to Richard.

7 What Tony can give Richard Nine of Swords

At first glance, this is an unfortunate card since it suggests that Tony can give Richard sleepless nights and worry, both of which he has already given in great measure. But it also shows that he can give him greater powers of discrimination, helping him to tell the difference between justifiable causes for concern and figments of his imagination.

8 What separates Tony from Richard
Queen of Swords

This card shows what separates Tony from Richard, and traditionally it refers to a widow: Elaine. Since Elaine also appeared in the set of cards referring to Richard, it is interesting to compare the two men's opinions of her. Tony evidently sees her as a woman who has endured a great deal of hardship and who now needs his support. Perhaps he is being over-protective of her, which is partly why he is so tough on Richard?

9 What unites Tony with Richard
Page of Pentacles

What unites Tony with Richard is Paul, Richard's younger brother. The Page of Pentacles can refer to a young man who is practical and mature for his age – this description fits Paul perfectly and it seems that he can act as a mediator between Tony and Richard. It is interesting that Paul is portrayed by a Pentacles card, as is Elaine in Richard's part of the spread. This echoing of cards is far more than a coincidence and suggests that the whole family is wrapped up in matters described by Pentacles, such as money, career and other materialistic factors.

10 Tony's greatest gift to Richard The Star

This card suggests that Tony's greatest gift to Richard is something that will bring Richard pleasure and spiritual nourishment, so it sounds as though there is a lot more to come out of their relationship. Tony may even enable Richard to make a dream come true, or to bring a creative project to fruition.

11 The karmic lesson Richard teaches Tony
Two of Cups

The karmic lesson that Richard is teaching Tony is to be able to forget their differences and forge an alliance. There is a sense of communion with this card, hinting at a deep and significant relationship that has yet to unfold between the two men.

12 The karmic lesson Tony teaches Richard
Five of Cups

The karmic lesson that Tony is teaching Richard is to concentrate on what he has salvaged from the situation rather than what he has lost. Instead of being full of regret and nostalgia for when his father was alive, he must concentrate on the present and try to benefit from it in some way.

the horseshoe spread

This is an excellent choice when you want to examine a situation in detail and see exactly what is going on. It is a classic, traditional spread so, as you would imagine, you will find variations of it in other books, with different meanings assigned to different cards. This variation, however, works very well.

Kathy was having tremendous problems with Gerald, a work colleague. She is a highly experienced waitress who, at the time of the reading, had recently begun a new job in a prestigious hotel. She was thrilled because the post represented a promotion and was well paid. At first, she really enjoyed herself, got on well with all the staff and her immediate boss was pleased with her work. However, after a couple of months Kathy began to have run-ins with Gerald, one of the chefs in the hotel kitchen. He claimed that she was making mistakes with her orders and also that she was stirring up trouble among the staff. He was rude to her virtually every day and, Kathy suspected, was spreading malicious rumours about her. She said she responded by ridiculing him behind his back. Kathy thought that the problems stemmed from Gerald's resentment of her after she stood up to him during a staff dispute and was supported by her boss. By the time she came for the reading, the situation had become so strained that she was having difficulty sleeping. She was also wondering whether to look for another job.

When analysing the spread, there are two Major Arcana cards, which is an average number in a spread of seven cards. The most notable feature of the spread is that there are three Cups cards, indicating that Kathy's emotions are working very powerfully. It would help if she could adopt a more objective view of the situation.

1 Past influences Nine of Cups

This card shows how well everything was going when Kathy first started at the hotel. She was happy and contented, pleased that she had landed such a good job and confident that it would work out well. The Nine of Cups carries plenty of promise, although sometimes reality falls short of our expectations, as it did here.

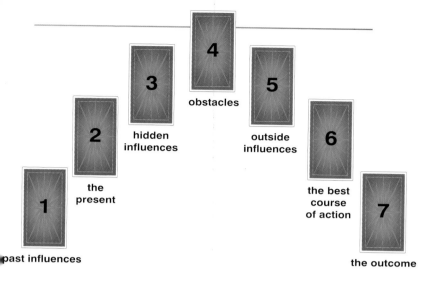

the present

hidden
influences

obstacles

outside
influences

the best
course
of action

past influences

the outcome

2 **The present** Two of Wands

The Two of Wands is encouraging Kathy to review her current
circumstances with as much detachment and objectivity as
possible. It often refers to a working partnership, so is of
particular interest in this spread. It suggests that Kathy might be
able to forge an alliance with someone at work, such as her
immediate boss or another colleague. This would help to reduce
the emotional charge of the situation.

3 **Hidden influences** Judgement

This card often appears in readings about disputes. It indicates that
one or both parties has been too quick to judge the other, and they
therefore need to examine the situation in a more forgiving light.
Here, in the position of hidden influences, Judgement is describing
the attitudes of both Kathy and Gerald. They both think that the
other one is to blame, and nothing will be resolved while this
continues. When we talked about this card's message of the need
to forgive others and to do one's best not to judge them, Kathy said
she would not forgive Gerald because it was all his fault. Our
conversation went round in circles.

4 **Obstacles** The Magician

The Magician describes someone with great power and
influence, and here it clearly refers to Gerald. It is a card
associated with trickery, so in this position it suggests that Gerald
is fanning the flames of the dispute by spreading false stories

4
obstacles
The Magician

3
hidden influences
Judgement

2
the present
Two of Wands

1
past influences
Nine of Cups

about Kathy and she should be very careful when dealing with him because he is clearly tricky. Nevertheless, retaliating through ridicule may only make the problem worse as such behaviour also comes under the domain of the Magician. This echoes the message of Judgement.

5 Outside influences Seven of Swords

Never an easy card, the Seven of Swords suggests that a third party may be contributing to the problem by telling untruths or doing something underhand. Kathy wondered if this was Gerald's good friend in the kitchen, who was also hostile towards her. No matter who this person is, Kathy needs to be careful about what she says and does, to ensure it does not give anyone further ammunition against her.

6 The best course of action Knight of Cups

This card is giving Kathy three messages: to concentrate on more pleasant areas of her life; to consider changing jobs;

5
outside influences
Seven of Swords

6
**the best course
of action**
Knight of Cups

7
the outcome
Ten of Cups

and to do whatever she feels is right. She admitted that she
had allowed herself to become fixated on the problems at
work, and that as a result she was neglecting some of her
leisure pursuits. The card's suggestion that she change jobs
echoed her own thoughts that this might well be a sensible
course of action. The Knight of Cups can also describe a
change of residence, and it turned out that Kathy was thinking
about moving to a different town and starting a new life there.

7 The outcome Ten of Cups

The Ten of Cups underlines the suggestion that it might be time
for Kathy to change jobs and, possibly, to move home as well.
This is one of the most favourable cards in the entire tarot,
because it describes happiness and fulfilment. As soon as Kathy
understood the message of this card, her mind was made up. On
her way home from the reading she visited an employment
agency and, three months later, she rang to say that she was now
living and working in a seaside town where she was very content.

the pyramid spread

Friendship can be wonderful: a delight and a source of sustenance when we have friends who are supportive, loving and emotionally generous. Yet most of us have experienced at least one friendship that started well but eventually became disappointing or hurtful. We might find that we are in some form of competition with our friend, we have little in common with them any longer or they are not the person we once knew. Yet, for old time's sake, we feel unable to break away from them.

Mark came for a reading at a difficult point in his relationship with John, who until recently he had always regarded as his best friend. They first met when they were both seven, and they went through school together. Although they attended different universities, they always stayed in close contact. Things started to change when they reached their mid-twenties and their lives began to go in completely different directions. Mark trained as a homeopath and John became a commodities broker. At first the differences did not matter but the gap has continued to widen between them. They are now both in their early forties.

Despite their busy lives, they manage to meet at least twice a month, but Mark no longer enjoys these encounters because he feels that John has changed into someone he does not like. John seems virtually obsessed with money, status and power. He also dominates most of the conversations, either talking about his latest purchases or his battles with his boss. Mark says that he sometimes feels like a piece of wallpaper as John holds forth: it seems that John is no longer interested in him as a person, merely as a captive audience. Mark asked for a reading because he wanted to know whether this was only a temporary phase or something more permanent. Listening to Mark talk, I was reminded that, sometimes, the phrase 'he is my best friend and I hate him' contains a great deal of truth!

The Pyramid Spread has a long tradition and has appeared in many different guises over the centuries. Sometimes you will see it with fewer cards, but this spread of twenty-one cards allows you to examine a situation in

8

recen
pas

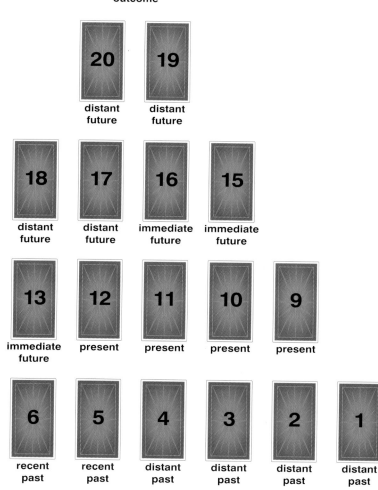

tremendous detail. It is ideal for Mark's dilemma because it scrutinises the past, present and future of his relationship with John, and also shows the outcome of the situation. It is not a spread for a beginner because it can be daunting to interpret so many cards in one go. However, it is an excellent choice when you begin to feel more confident.

It can take some time to gain an overview of this spread because there are so many cards to assess. Here, there are five Major Arcana cards, which is below the average number you would expect to see, so matters are very much in Mark's hands. There are three Swords, five Cups, four

Wands and four Pentacles, which makes a good overall balance of the suits. The presence of three Aces is very notable, especially as they all belong to the category of the distant past. Unfortunately, the card describing the outcome was far from encouraging. However, it is a valuable reminder that the events foretold in a reading may not come true if the warnings contained in the spread are heeded.

1 Distant past Ace of Cups

When John and Mark first met, their relationship meant a great deal to both of them. They

21
outcom
Ten of Sw

20
distant future
The Hierophan

18
distant future
Four of Swords

17
distant future
The Chariot

14
immediate future
Knight of Cups

13
immediate future
Eight of Wands

12
present
Queen of Sword

8
recent past
Four of Wands

7
recent past
Eight of Pentacles

6
recent past
Five of Cups

5
recent past
Four of Cups

developed a strong emotional bond. Mark
said that when they were eight they swore
that they would be blood brothers for ever,
and even performed a special ceremony
based on a ritual they read about in a book.

2 Distant past King of Cups

This card underlines the meaning of the Ace
of Cups, showing that the friendship allowed
both boys to display their emotions and to
enjoy the powerful links between them.
It was obviously a very important
relationship for both of them.

19
distant future
ve of Pentacles

16
immediate future
The World

15
immediate future
The Star

11
present
vo of Pentacles

10
present
Six of Wands

9
present
The Devil

4
distant past
ce of Pentacles

3
distant past
Ace of Wands

2
distant past
King of Cups

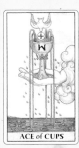

1
distant past
Ace of Cups

3 **Distant past** Ace of Wands

The Ace of Wands describes the excitement that Mark felt when he began to train as a homeopath. He said it opened many doors for him and encouraged him to see the world in a completely different way. He felt he was part of something much greater than himself, and he absolutely loved it.

4 **Distant past** Ace of Pentacles

The Ace of Pentacles can be read in two ways here: as further emphasis of the importance of the friendship for both boys, and also as the start of an enterprise involving money or other material benefits. It clearly refers to John's financial training and the subsequent career that blossomed for him.

5 **Recent past** Four of Cups

This is a card of dissatisfaction and discontent. Mark felt it described John's recent change of attitude from being someone who was always interested in life to one who seemed world-weary and jaded. He said John was always looking for new, bigger thrills because the old ones palled so quickly.

6 **Recent past** Five of Cups

Mark's sense of loss caused by the change in their friendship is described perfectly here. However, it is telling him to focus on what he has salvaged from the relationship rather than what has gone. He said he found this difficult because he was so unhappy about it. It was obvious that he was also very angry.

7 **Recent past** Eight of Pentacles

The Eight of Pentacles encourages us to develop our talents and to be proud of them. When we discussed this, Mark said that John had begun to make derisory comments about homeopathy and Mark's other interests, implying that they were somehow foolish because they did not bring in stacks of money.

8 **Recent past** Four of Wands

One of the classic meanings of the Four of Wands is a change of residence. Mark said John had recently moved, and was now living in an extremely expensive house on which he was spending vast amounts of money. Mark sounded slightly envious of this, although he denied it vehemently.

9 Present The Devil

This card represents the nub of the problem: a sense of enslavement. To some degree, Mark is enslaved to his happy memories of the friendship and all that it means to him, while John seems enslaved to material values and a lavish way of living. Both of them need to find some sort of compromise.

10 Present Six of Wands

The Six of Wands describes the triumph and acclaim that comes with success. Mark said it referred to the expansion that was taking place in his homeopathic practice, with the arrival of several new clients and the invitation to work at a local doctor's surgery twice a week. This is something to celebrate and Mark should give himself due credit for it, no matter what John might have to say on the subject.

11 Present Two of Pentacles

Normally, this card describes a need to balance one's finances or energy, but here it clearly shows the discrepancy between the two men's financial situations and the difficulties this is causing. Their circumstances are linked, so John's material wealth makes Mark feel impoverished, even though this is not really the case.

12 Present Queen of Swords

The woman described by the Queen of Swords is often a widow or someone who has endured some difficult times, and Mark said it referred to John's divorced mother who had recently become ill and was waiting for an operation. Mark is very close to her, describing her as his second mother, and is concerned about her. He said that she was one of the reasons he was reluctant to end his friendship with John, because he did not know if she would still want to see him if that happened. Here is another example of the ties described by the Devil.

13 **Immediate future** Eight of Wands

Life often becomes very busy when the Eight of Wands appears, especially if travel is involved. Mark said that he, John and their partners had been considering going on holiday together, although this would have to be arranged at the last minute to tie in with the date for John's mother's operation.

14 **Immediate future** Knight of Cups

This is an intriguing card in this position because it describes the importance of following one's heart and doing what will make one happy. Mark should enjoy his interests even if John is not impressed by them. The card can also indicate an opportunity, especially if it is linked to travel. It therefore suggests that if the projected holiday goes ahead it will be very enjoyable. It may also bring Mark and John closer together.

15 **Immediate future** The Star

Here is another card that encourages one to follow one's heart. It also promises that difficult situations will improve, which bodes well for the friendship. The Star carries another interesting message that seems very relevant, which is not to take a polarised view of problems but to find a balanced way of dealing with them. Perhaps Mark is being too critical of John? He accepted that this might well be true.

16 **Immediate future** The World

This card was further confirmation that the holiday would go ahead. It also indicated that this would lead to a change of attitude on someone's part, and that it would have a big effect on the friendship. The World can indicate the end of one cycle and the start of another, so will the friendship enter a more positive phase or come to an end?

17 **Distant future** The Chariot

The Chariot often indicates a difficult time, with the need to stick it out until things get better. Very often this involves plenty of willpower and the determination not to seek one's revenge as it will only lead to more trouble. It therefore seems that the problems in the friendship are not yet completely resolved.

18 **Distant future** Four of Swords

The Four of Swords describes the need for a rest after a stressful interlude. Since this reading revolves around the friendship between Mark and John, it suggests that their relationship will encounter more difficulties in the future and that Mark will have to take stock of the situation, which may involve withdrawing for a while so he can think things through.

19 **Distant future** Five of Pentacles

This is never an easy card because it describes the potential loss of something very valuable. Here, it sounds a strong warning that the situation between Mark and John is likely to degenerate still further unless they both do something constructive about it. But will they?

20 **Distant future** The Hierophant

The Hierophant is reminding Mark not to take the moral high ground, nor to assume that the problems in the relationship are all one-sided. It also warns against placing people on pedestals, suggesting that either Mark or John expects too much from the other one. They must both be realistic and pragmatic.

21 **Outcome** Ten of Swords

This is one of the worst possible outcomes for a reading, since it speaks of endings and possible betrayal. However, it might describe the end of a particular phase in their friendship, rather than the end of the friendship itself. I reassured Mark that the difficult message of the Ten of Swords will not necessarily be the outcome if both he and John are prepared to make adjustments and to heed the warnings of the cards that describe the distant future.

index

240